FEMINISM AND
FAMILY PLANNING
IN VICTORIAN ENGLAND

Studies in the Life of Women

Feminism and Family Planning in Victorian England

J. A. and OLIVE BANKS

SCHOCKEN BOOKS · NEW YORK

Contents

Introduction

THE control of population growth is widely recognized to be one of the major issues facing the world at the present time. Anxiety at the rapidity with which the world's population is increasing is dwarfed only by fears that the nuclear arms race will end in the destruction of humanity itself. Yet, in spite of this general recognition of the gravity of this problem, efforts to stem the tide of births in what are frequently known as the over-populated countries have met, so far, with very little success. It is sometimes argued that since the decline in the birth-rate in Europe is a consequence of industrialization and urbanization, the spread of industry to the 'under-developed' countries will lead in its own time to a fall in family size. It has also been argued that as the rise of feminism coincided with the fall of the birth-rate in England, the relationship between the two was a causal one, and it has been somewhat rashly concluded from this that feminist movements should be encouraged in 'over-populated' areas with the object of restricting the growth of population. While the proposition, that industrialization brings with it the small family, may be true, the 'wait and see' policy sometimes based on it can, at best, only be regarded as a very long term solution of the problem. The latter proposition, that feminism also leads to a reduction in size of families is, as will be seen, highly questionable. It is easy to demonstrate that there was not only a considerable time-lag between the first stages in industrialization and the acceptance of birth-control, but a further delay also occurred before the practice spread from the professional middle classes to other sections of the community. Moreover, so far as countries like India and China are concerned, it would seem that the progress of industrialization is itself hindered by the rate of population growth which must fall before industrialization can proceed.

There are, however, other differences which suggest the possibility of a more optimistic conclusion. In England, the birth-control movement had to fight against the opposition of both the Church and the medical profession, as well as the general run of people who thought of themselves as 'respectable', and that is one reason why it became linked to some extent in the public mind with feminism. In most of the 'under-developed' countries today the spread of birth-control knowledge is a matter of state policy, and while religious opinion is divided on the various methods of contraception, there is no opposition to the idea of family planning to meet the threat of over-population.[1] The problem, therefore, is to discover ways of arousing the desire for a smaller family in those countries and those classes where such a desire has not yet arisen, and it is in this context that a further study of the voluntary decisions of the Victorian middle classes to adopt family limitation takes on more than an antiquarian interest.

It is not suggested here that a study of nineteenth-century England is a substitute for detailed investigation of the actual problems facing individual communities. Nevertheless, it is believed that there is still much to learn about the reasons for the nineteenth-century fall in fertility and that a clearer understanding of the precise mechanisms involved, apart from its undoubted theoretical interest, will also be of practical use in suggesting where the significant areas lie. Indeed, the main practical justification for an enquiry couched primarily in theoretical terms is precisely that it does enable us to distinguish between the significant and insignificant, and to differentiate clearly between what is purely a coincidence in time and what is a genuine relationship between events which occur together. This is especially true in the present case, because of the fact that over the past hundred years the status of women has risen and the fertility of women has declined, so that it is tempting to think of them as causally related; and this gives any study of the two phenomena a special relevance at the present time, since the women of the less economically advanced nations are certainly experiencing changes in their status which some observers have concluded must necessarily result in a reduction of the size of their families; and hence the solution to the popu-

1. See for example, *The Family in Contemporary Society*, S.P.C.K., 1958, a report prepared by a group convened by the Church of England Moral Welfare Council.

lation problem will arise automatically from measures not directly designed for that end.

A study of feminism and family planning in Victorian England, therefore, can be of value for contemporary population policy makers in so far as it makes clear the extent to which there is a necessary connection between the aims of family planners and the particular means which they have chosen to achieve them; but it may also be of value for those who are concerned to raise the status of women, all over the world, as an end in itself. It could hardly be claimed that all the ideals which the pioneers of the movement and the champions of its heyday held so clearly before themselves have been achieved. All over the world, it is true, women have been and are being admitted to equal citizenship rights with men, to equal opportunities for participating in schools and universities, and to widening fields of employment, but in many ways a double standard still exists.[2] Discrimination on grounds of sex may no longer be operated institutionally, exceptional cases apart, but often a tacit understanding exists that women *per se* are not so fitted as men to play a major part in decisive affairs in industry, politics or religion, and even in the world of art or sport their position is ambiguous. The questions which arise for practical reformers, accordingly, are, should the status of women be raised by people working *on their behalf* or will such measures be of no avail, without corresponding efforts by women themselves to claim their rights? Again, we should hesitate to make a simple application of the conclusions to be derived from a study of Victorian England to developments elsewhere at the present time, but it does seem reasonable to claim that a study which shows how an organized movement, feminism, is related to a parallel development, the emancipation of women, has considerable practical relevance in that it distinguishes between reforms which have been and may be achieved by direct organized action, and social changes which

2. A very clear example, and one which recalls to mind the controversies of the late nineteenth century in a very immediate way, is the attitude taken towards prostitution by the Report of the Committee on Homosexual Offences and Prostitution, which has since been embodied in legislation imposing penalties on prostitutes rather than their customers, with the aim of 'keeping the streets clean'.

are the unintended and unanticipated consequences of events in areas of human activity somewhat removed from the centre of the controversy.

The significance of this last point should not be missed. Although this present study is primarily an enquiry into family planning, and although its secondary concern is with feminism and the emancipation of women, its practical implications are not necessarily limited to these fields alone. In almost every sphere of human activity reformers are presented with the problem sooner or later of deciding which of their goals are practical possibilities and which must be left to the logic of events to solve themselves. Eventually, all organized movements begin to flag, and means are sought to revitalize them. This has been the case with feminism, but it is also true of many other attempts at social reform, not excepting the Labour Party at the present time. Of course, it is not suggested that practical solutions to such problems emerge directly from a study of this kind. That would be an absurd claim. Nevertheless, it is clear that mere exhortation to remember the ideals of the founders is no substitute for genuine enquiry into causes and conditions. A study of feminism, that is to say, should not be dismissed as dealing with an outmoded issue of interest only to students of Victoriana. It has implications also for those who are concerned with the fortunes of widely different movements.

This, indeed, is one very good reason why the present tendency to dismiss the whole subject of feminism as trivial is to be deplored and why a more detailed treatment than has been possible here is an urgent necessity at the present time. It is to be hoped that this general examination of the problems that arise will encourage other students to regard it as a case study of the relationship between social movements and social change, and to add to our knowledge by carrying out further studies in this neglected field of sociological study. For it is true that, in general, we know very little about the relation between the social policies embodied in such movements, the social conditions of their time and social change generally. The last two generations of sociologists have, as has recently been pointed out, given such questions 'remarkably little serious attention'. 'Text-books in sociology . . . often relegate discussions of social change to a final chapter, or sometimes to a small section located well to the rear of numerous chapters on culture, socialization, social groups, and the community . . . the study of social change has become something of a part-time concern in recent years . . . The essential anomaly is that [it] . . . has become a speciality without specialists.'³

3. Alvin Boskoff, 'Social Change: Major Problems in the Emergence of Theoretical and Research Foci', in Howard Becker and Alvin Boskoff, *Modern Sociological Theory in Continuity and Change*, The Dryden Press, 1957, pp. 260–1.

FEMINISM AND
FAMILY PLANNING
IN VICTORIAN ENGLAND

CHAPTER 1

Fertility and the Feminine Protest

ACCOUNTS of political and industrial revolutions excite the imagination with the violence of their impact on the men and women of their time, but the long-term social results of many less impressive institutional changes are no less significant, even if they cannot be described in such dramatic terms. This is particularly true of the family revolution of the twentieth century in the western world. As compared with the mid-Victorian era when a large number of children was regarded as the inevitable consequence of a marriage, most people today regard the small, deliberately planned family as the normal order of things; and the effect of this on the pattern of social relationships we call 'society' has been as far-reaching as those other, more striking events which have so often received the attention of the popular historian.

To the sociologist, moreover, a mere chronicle of the events in the history of this flight from parenthood is unsatisfactory; there must be some attempt at explanation. Thus, while it is fairly well-established that the movement towards family limitation did not really begin until the 1870's and then amongst the wealthier sections of the community primarily, what is interesting is how it came about that the new reproductive habits which only later spread to the less privileged social groups, first came to be established among the families of professional and business men.[1] What social factors were responsible for this change of outlook on life? All kinds of suggestions have been put forward, including a 'complex web, rather than a chain, of cause and effect'[2] covering most of the social and industrial developments which were characteristic of the nineteenth century. Speculation in this field is commonplace. The question

---

1. *The Census of England and Wales, 1911*, Vol. 13. *Fertility and Marriage*, Part I (1917). J. W. Innes, *Class Fertility Trends in England and Wales, 1876–1934* (1938), Ch. 3.

2. *Report of the Royal Commission on Population*, June, 1949. *Parliamentary Papers* (1948–9), Vol. 19, para. 96.

is: how far can we move from speculation to a more systematic, and sociologically satisfactory, analysis of the family planning ideas of the Victorian upper-middle class?

Some attempt has already been made to do this. Arguing that 'an empirical investigation which tried to carry along every conceivable influence upon the fall in fertility would become tediously involved and complicated' and that, therefore, some selection among suggested influence is necessary, a single 'manageable' factor was isolated for study in the hope that once the precise nature of its part in the fall in fertility was known we should 'be better able to consider the relative importance of other possible contributing influences.'[3] This factor was the rising standard of living, an economic concept shown to entail two logically distinct ideas, (1) an increase in the actual material well-being of a class of people, and (2) an expansion in the range of satisfactions which they considered appropriate for a civilized existence. As far as the available evidence would permit, the content of the Victorian middle-class standard of living was determined in these terms and related to what could be ascertained about developments in opinion on the propriety of family planning and birth-control. The study, thereupon, concluded with the view that:

the argument that the rising standard of living was the *major* factor in the spread of family limitation, although strongly supported by a plausible array of evidence, must remain something of a *non sequitur*. . . . Some of the alternative variables in the web of causal factors must now be followed through, such as the breakdown of the family as an economic unit, the growth of urban living, the decline in religious belief, or the emancipation of women. In this way we may yet be enabled to assign a relative weight to each of the suggested causes under review, and in the course of time be able to discern which of them, if any, has performed the most fundamental part in the fall in fertility.[4]

It is important that this conclusion should be fully understood. *Prosperity and Parenthood* may be legitimately read as evidence for the view that the rising standard of living is a *necessary* condition for the adoption of family-planning ideas. Without a rising

3. J. A. Banks, *Prosperity and Parenthood, a study of family planning among the Victorian middle classes* (1954), pp. 8 and 11.
4. *Ibid.*, pp. 202 and 207. Italics in the original.

standard of living, birth-control propaganda will fail to have any marked effect on social habits. But *Prosperity and Parenthood* may not be read as evidence for the view that a rising standard of living automatically and inevitably results in a decline in family size. Other features of change in the England of the 1860's and 1870's, such as the successes of the growing feminist movements, or the spread of secularist ideas, the growth of towns or the widespread separation of home from work, may have been equally necessary conditions for the acceptance of Neo-Malthusian views at that time. Only if it can be shown that people have been mistaken in attributing influence to these changes, or that even if these changes have been influential they themselves were the inevitable results of the rising standard of living, may it be validly argued that the rising standard of living is not only a necessary but a *sufficient* condition for the advent of the smaller family. In taking up any of these further possible factors for study, therefore, we should seek to ascertain their relationship both to family planning and to the standard of living.

The method used in *Prosperity and Parenthood*, of course, implies more than this. It implies that although we are aware that the number of suggested factors is quite large, we should curb our impatience and study them one at a time. It is not our intention here to present a methodological justification for this approach, other than in terms of its relative simplicity and convenience. Indeed, we might as well admit that at the present stage of sociological sophistication there is little more that we can do, if the work of empirical investigation is to proceed at all. Unless we are content to wait until a logically satisfying method for the study of social change is evolved, we must go ahead with what tools of analysis we have, trusting that in the course of time our findings will prove useful to later generations of sociologists with more refined techniques for historical study at their command. In the present instance, for example, it would be gratifying to know how it is possible to evaluate the 'precise nature' of the part played by any factor in the retreat from parenthood. Full possession of all the data about the thoughts and actions of those people who began to practise birth-control in the 1870's might have made this possible, but even a cursory glance through the literature on the Victorian middle-

class concept of the ideal family size will serve to show what
little 'precision' exists in this field. Our reading of the material
must perforce be interpretive and what we must do, if we are
to escape the charge of obscurantism, is to provide a full docu-
mentary of our sources of information so that those who desire
to challenge our results may freely use the material accessible
to us. In no other way does it seem at present that the systematic and disciplined approach of sociology can be applied
to the study of social change where the data has been recorded,
but not for sociological purposes, in the past.

But there is another reason for studying factors one at a time,
other than the sheer difficulty of obtaining precision in each of
many. *Prosperity and Parenthood* was written in the context of
'variable' theories of social change. Such theories assume, for
the purpose of investigation and explanation, that wherever
several factors are involved in some enquiry it makes sense to
think of some as more influential than others and of some as
working in different directions from others. Not content with
lists of necessary conditions for the social phenomenon with
which they are concerned, theorists of this persuasion seek to
assign relative weights to these conditions so that they may distinguish between the major and minor, the more important
and the less important influence in the shaping of some massive
historical event. To obtain precision in such circumstances is
no easy matter, and our task would become Herculean were
we to take a number of suggested variables and attempt to
assess their relative influence in a single exercise. On the other
hand, were we to investigate the influence of every factor
separately, we should be faced eventually not solely with the
problem of determining their manner of inter-acting but also
with that of deciding on the degree of precision involved in our
knowledge of each. Our compromise is to study each newly
chosen factor in terms of our knowledge of the one that has
gone before and in this way make preliminary assignments of
relative significance as we proceed. This alternative, to be sure,
pre-supposes that the data on inter-action is no less precise
than those on the several factors considered above, but for the
purposes of the present enquiry such an assumption has had to
suffice. Hence in turning to consider a second likely 'cause'
of the Victorian retreat from frequent child bearing, we have

attempted both to trace the effect of feminism on attitudes towards marriage and family size, and to examine in what ways it is related to changes in middle-class standards of living.

This raises the question of why this particular topic was selected as the second for study. In *Prosperity and Parenthood* the choice of the economic factor was justified on the ground of a widespread tendency to stress it as the element of greatest importance.[5] Both in the history of population literature from Malthus onwards.[6] and in a sample enquiry made for the Royal Commission on Population,[7] considerations of cost have been regularly advanced as the major reason for resorting to some kind of family limitation. A similar claim might be made for the present theme. Quite apart from listing feminism and the growing independence of women as one of the strands in a great web of social forces, the revolt of women has been accorded the most significant place in the domestic revolution of our time.[8] 'That the drop in birth-rates is due especially to the spread of knowledge among women cannot be doubted. Men had it already, but seldom acted upon it when they married.'[9] But such a claim for the priority of feminism is rare, and does not in any case justify in itself its selection as the next most significant factor worth investigating. Other hypotheses may have their champions, too, and to select any one merely because some writer has put it forward is a procedure of very doubtful validity.

It is, however, the case that child-bearing and child-rearing usually weigh more heavily on wives than on their husbands, so that it is not unreasonable *a priori* to assume that a change in their willingness to perform these duties might well have been

5. J. A. Banks, *op. cit.*, pp. 8 and 9.

6. *Ibid.*, Ch. 2 and Note A to Ch. 1, p. 218. J. Field, *Essays on Population and Other Papers* (1931) and K. Smith, *The Malthusian Controversy* (1951).

7. E. Lewis-Faning, *Family Limitation and its Influence on Human Fertility during the past Fifty Years* (1949). Papers of the Royal Commission on Population, Vol. 1, Ch. 12, especially tables 123 and 125.

8. N. Himes, *The Medical History of Contraception* (1934), Ch. 13, para 6. *Population Policy in Great Britain: a Report by P.E.P.* (April, 1948), pp. 5 and 75. *Report of the Royal Commission on Population*, paras. 96 and 103.

9. H. Fyfe, *Revolt of Women* (1933), p. 12. His further argument that the revolt began in France (p. 81) has been separately advanced by P. Aries, in 'Sur les origines de la contraception en France', in *Population*, Juillet-Sept., 1953, Vol. 8, No. 3, pp. 471–2.

a salient factor in the acceptance of birth-control ideas. Fyfe, for example, has argued that in addition to characteristic differences between the sexes in the matter of planning and looking ahead generally, men have no obvious interest in the size of their families since they are not required to bear the children and 'few of them have the least idea what discomfort and pain mothers endure, or of the dangers they go through.'[10] There is certainly some evidence for the existence among wealthier women in the first half of the nineteenth century of a desire for relief from the burden of child-bearing, although mixed with a strong streak of fatalism.

I think, dearest Uncle, you cannot *really* wish me to be the 'Mamma d'une nombreuse famille', for I think you will see with me the great inconvenience a *large* family would be to us all, and particularly to the country, independent of the hardship and inconvenience to myself: men never think; at least seldom think, what a hard task it is for us women to go through this *very often*. God's will be done, and if He decrees that we are to have a great number of children, why we must try to bring them up as useful and exemplary members of society.[11]

Yet it would hardly seem necessary to depend on *a priori* arguments for a changed outlook on the part of women to translate their 'latent desire to be delivered from this burden' of child-birth and child-rearing[12] into positive action to prevent too many and too frequent births, when the appearance on the historical scene in Britain of organized movements to propagate family planning and organized movements on behalf of the emancipation of women coincided so closely in time. The establishment of the first Malthusian League by Charles Bradlaugh and the publication of articles on the urgent need for birth-control in his *National Reformer*, the participation of women in the Congresses of the Association for the Promotion of Social

---

10. *Op. cit.*, p. 12.

11. Letter from Queen Victoria to the King of the Belgians, 5 January, 1841, reproduced in A. C. Benson and Viscount Ester, *The Letters of Queen Victoria: a Selection from Her Majesty's Correspondence between the years 1837 and 1861* (1907), Vol. I, p. 321. Italics in the original.

12. A. M. Carr-Saunders, *World Population, Past Growth and Present Trends*, Clarendon, Oxford, 1936, p. 107. In Carr-Saunders' view it was 'the presence of moral sentiments, opposed to the discussion and even more to the employment of contraceptives, which kept women in bondage to the large family'.

Science, their demand for opportunities in education, for employment outside the traditional callings of domestic servant and governess, for permission to enter the established professions, and for the vote, are all a feature of the 1860's. Many years were to pass, of course, before either of these movements swung public opinion around to their way of thinking but it seems clear that their progress in that direction was matched step by step so that we find, for example, in the same decade that women were granted formal political equality, there were opened birth-control clinics as public places where information about family planning and contraceptives might be easily obtained.

The possibility that the two movements were causally linked has, therefore, a certain plausibility which demands further investigation. It has in addition very definite practical implications. For those parts of the world where the idea of birth-control is still struggling for popular acceptance alongside attempts to raise the status of women, it is of some moment to ascertain whether the general spread of birth-control techniques is necessarily dependent upon a prior change in the legal, political and domestic position of women, whether the two are independent of one another, or indeed, as yet a third possibility, whether the emancipation of women must wait upon a reduction in family size. It is not suggested that this study, by itself, can provide the answer to these fundamental questions, at least in this general form in which they are usually put. Nevertheless, it will provide some of the material upon which such answers must be based by providing evidence for or against the view that feminism is a necessary condition for the acceptance of family planning and by showing the relationship between the two movements and changes in the standard of living.

Perhaps the most impelling inducement for a study of feminism in Britain, however, is the intrinsic attraction of investigating a subject about which so much has been written and so little of sociological value has been said. Histories of the feminist movement are rarely more than accounts of the path towards emancipation.[13] More detailed investigations are usually

13. See, for example, Ray Strachey, *The Cause: a Short History of the Women's Movement in Great Britain*, Bell, London, 1928.

biographies of the movement's most outstanding figures. Sociological treatment of the internal dynamics of the movement and of their relation to other developments in the society of their time are non-existent.[14] Little or no attempt has been made to explain even its most glaring failures of achievement. While it is true to say that the sociology of social movements is in its infancy in any case, it is, nevertheless, surprising that the subject of feminism has not been tackled before this, as providing interesting data in its own right as well as being sufficiently manageable for slender resources. The lack of a proper social enquiry into the movement has, indeed, proved a bugbear in the present instance, and although it cannot be claimed that anything more than an initial and, by its very nature, partial study of feminism has been included in this investigation into family planning in Victorian England, it is to be hoped that it will encourage others to carry the subject further, as well as throwing some light itself on 'one of the most striking aspects of the industrial phase of social development.'[15]

We should, perhaps, issue the warning that it is important to be clear about what is to be understood by 'feminism' in this context. At one level we may think of it as a set of doctrines which have been developed over the past 150 years on the place of women in society, and more especially, on the extent to which women should have equal rights, opportunities and responsibilities with those of men. These doctrines are associated with the names of people such as Mary Wollstonecroft, William Thompson and John Stuart Mill, to mention three of the most famous of the early feminists. John Stuart Mill is particularly outstanding because of his prestige as one of the foremost liberal thinkers of his time, and his influence, both as a liberal and a feminist, extended very widely. It has been suggested, for example, that Mill's *Subjection of Women* was the main inspira-

14. An exception is to be found in Part II, Ch. 3 of George Dangerfield's *The Strange Death of Liberal England*, Constable, London, 1936. Roger Fulford's *Votes for Women, the Story of a Struggle*, Faber and Faber, 1957, is a mere chronicle in comparison.

15. O. R. McGregor, 'The Social Position of Women in England, 1850–1914: a Bibliography', *The British Journal of Sociology*, Vol. 6, No. 1, March, 1955. McGregor finds 'equally striking' its present neglect.   'It has neither attracted comprehensive sociological analysis nor acquired status as an established theme of the history books. It is not a subject on which men or women easily find their way to rational views.'

tion of Japanese writings on the subject.[16] Feminism, in this sense of an ideology, was primarily a creation of the nineteenth century and it is noteworthy that later feminist writers such as Olive Schreiner, Virginia Woolf and Vera Brittain, while appealing to a partly emancipated generation of women and dealing with very different practical problems, continue to repeat Mill's plea for an end to the subjection of women by men.

It is precisely because of this emphasis on equality between the sexes that feminism must not be assumed necessarily to entail the idea of birth-control. The large family need not be seen as a disability weighing more heavily on the woman than on the man, or indeed as imposed upon her by him. Certainly the advocates of family planning did not see the issue in this light and addressed their appeals equally to both sexes. It was only a few feminists who regarded the smaller family as providing opportunities for a wider emancipation of women and hence as a means to equality; and, as we shall see, in so far as a discussion was provoked on the relationship between the sexes, it did not turn on this question at all but on the biological and social basis for inequality.

But, the writings of men like John Stuart Mill and women like Olive Schreiner do not exhaust the whole concept of feminism. Of even greater significance for our purpose is the organized movement which sought, not always successfully, to translate doctrine into reality. It is possible to think of this in two ways. On the one hand we may look at the attempts of ardent men and women to prevail upon parliament to change the law with respect to the property of married women, or to induce the universities to admit girls as undergraduates, or to persuade the professions to accept qualified women on equal terms with men, and we may examine whether a case for, or against birth-control was put forward on any feminist platform during the crucial years when opinion may be said to have been forming on this issue. The answer to this question would not appear to present any special difficulties and we may say that so far as we can tell, family-planning propaganda played no

16. Baroness Shidzué Ishimota, *Facing Two Ways*, Cassell, London, 1935, pp. 369–70.

part in the demands of the feminist movement until the fall in
the size of the family was already well under way.

On the other hand, it is not sufficient to stop at the appearance
which the feminists themselves believed they were giving to the
world. We have to enquire whether the impression of them which
was recognized by the people of their day, included not only
features of orthodox feminism but those of neo-Malthusianism.
The evidence for this latter enquiry is not so simple to obtain
or to interpret, but on the whole we may say that the anti-
feminists, at any rate, while seeing many undesirable consequences in the efforts of the reformers, such as a retreat from
marriage altogether on the part of single women with a career,
and the neglect of their homes on the part of married women
who tried to combine both, at no time included birth-control
amongst them. Publicly, attacks on feminism were not linked
with attacks on family planning. Of course, we have no means
of telling what the anti-feminists thought privately, especially
as their biographies, letters and diaries are silent on the issue;
nor do we know what those who were indifferent to feminism
believed, although this at least we can claim, that those who
were indifferent can hardly be said to have been influenced
directly, either one way or the other, by the movement to change
the position of women in society.

Feminism, then, may be seen to include literary men and
women advocating sex equality, and organized bodies of active
workers for the cause, and when we think of it as a movement
embracing both we may have in mind not only their aims and
purposes, but the consequences of their efforts, intended and
unintended alike. The smaller family, as we have seen, was not
one of those things which the organized feminists originally
sought to achieve, but it may, nevertheless, have been provoked
by their achievements in other fields. This aspect of our enquiry clearly presents us with greater difficulties. Logically,
the argument that women had the right to take a greater
share of equality in social and domestic life, would seem to
imply that they should have an equal share with their husbands
in deciding the number of children to be born. Historically,
we have to ask whether family planning when it came, took
this form, and whether the efforts of the reformers had proceeded so far by the 1870's that a revolt of wives against their

husbands over the issue of conception, was a necessary consequence of the successes that had gone before. It must be admitted that evidence which would satisfy these queries is largely lacking, and all that we can do is to suggest that the weight of the evidence does not lend itself to such interpretations. The very nature of the feminist appeal during the crucial years before the 1870's—its emphasis on restricted problems, mostly of concern to unmarried women and widows—and especially the limited success of precisely those features of its programme which might conceivably have produced a revolution within the family, in the sense of a challenge to the husband's right to decide such matters as these, must be seen as evidence against the possibility of any such unintended and unanticipated consequences.

So far, we have been concerned with what we have described as feminism—the deliberate attempt to achieve equality between the sexes in the political, economic and domestic spheres. The concept of the emancipation of women, on the other hand, while containing the goals of feminism, and its successes, may be said to have a wider meaning. The nineteenth century saw many changes in the lives of married women of the middle classes which were not part of feminism but which may properly be said to have emancipated them from the exclusively domestic role, which was theirs in the early years of the century. These changes which may be characterized as a transition from the perfect wife to the perfect lady, may not be attributed to feminism. The feminists, indeed, were hostile to them, as representing everything to which they were opposed. For the aim of the feminists was for women to play a useful and constructive part in society. They had no desire for them to become mere symbols of the male power conspicuously to consume, as Veblen put it. An ostentatious and expensive life of domestic leisure could hardly be mistaken for equality with men, at a time when ambition in a career and living productively in general were being stressed as virtues for the young men of the middle classes. Moreover, it is not at all obvious how this transition to the elegant lady of the 1870's could have been a consequence, however unknowing or unwilling, of feminist achievement. It is far more reasonable to look elsewhere for the cause.

It is here that we re-introduce the topic of the standard of living, as it was left at the end of *Prosperity and Parenthood*. Between 1850 and 1870 the growing prosperity of the middle and upper-middle classes expressed itself, not only in a more luxurious style of life but in a drive for social esteem. This took the form of displaying all the paraphernalia of gentility—large and expensive houses, numerous domestic servants employed outdoors as well as in, carriage and horses, fairly long holidays abroad, public school and university for the sons of the family, frequent and lavish dinner parties, and so on. Amongst such symbols of social status the transition from the perfect wife to the perfect lady was of crucial importance for the middle-class woman. There was, we might say, a repudiation of the purely domestic virtues precisely because of their association with a rather more lowly past. To the aspiring middle classes the kitchen was no place in which to demonstrate one's social prestige. The result was to emancipate the middle class women from the exclusively domestic role and to give her more leisure in which to indicate that the appropriate status symbols had been acquired. She thus began to enjoy a more varied social life.

Emancipation from the constraints of the domestic routine, however, should not be confused with emancipation from dependence upon the male members of the family. If anything, the changes of the prosperous decades of the nineteenth century, increased the middle-class woman's subservience by relegating her to the position of a status object. It was at this point that the transition from the perfect wife to the perfect lady, far from being produced by feminism, became a potent factor in producing it: for, the drive and energy of the leading members of the movement came from their release from the burden of domesticity on the one hand, and from revolt against what seemed to them to be the triviality and humiliation of what had taken its place, on the other. It is in this sense that the rising standard of living may be said to have been a causal factor in the development of feminism, acting not directly but through the intermediary of modifying the middle-class women's traditional domestic role.

There is, moreover, some evidence that this repudiation of domestic values—although by both sexes and not exclusively

by women—may have played its part in making the middle
classes of the 1870's receptive to the idea of the limitation of
family size. Children were no longer the rationale of a 'civilized'
woman's whole existence. Instead, they often seemed to be an
expensive liability and so had become a suitable subject for re-
trenchment, if and when this became a necessity. Rather than
give up the paraphernalia of gentility, including the leisured
and expensive lady of fashion, it became sound policy to postpone the birth of offspring. The study of the part played by the
rising standard of living in the transition from the perfect wife
and mother of the 1840's to the perfect lady of the 1870's,
therefore, is essential for filling a gap in our knowledge of the
relationship between the middle-class conception of a civilized
existence and family planning in the latter decades of the nineteenth century; and, as we shall see, the evidence which it is
possible to collect on this point strengthens the argument that
changes in the standard of living were a major factor in the
spread of birth-control ideas.

The significance of this conclusion, however, should not be
misunderstood. If all that the following chapters had to reveal
were further evidence on the causes of the decline in family
size in nineteenth-century England, they would add little to
what has already been argued, albeit inconclusively, in *Prosperity
and Parenthood*. But, in examining the relationship of feminism
to the birth-control movement, the aim has been to consider it
in a rather wider context than its bearing on family planning
alone. In particular, it has been a central concern that the
attitude of feminists to this and to related issues be regarded as
of considerable interest in and for itself. The very absence of
any definite feminist policy on family limitation is a fact which
urgently demands investigation. Unfortunately, the reticence of
the period on certain sexual matters, although not on all, makes
the task of explanation unusually difficult, but that is not an
adequate ground for not making the attempt. It would be idle,
of course, to pretend that more has been done here than to draw
attention to some curious and previously unexplored facets of
the feminist attitude towards sex. These may well have given the
movement its special qualities and have played their part in
producing both overt indifference to the goals of the neo-
Malthusians and possibly covert rejection of them. The justi-

fication for this study, therefore, is twofold. Not only does it seek to give a more positive answer than was possible at the end of *Prosperity and Parenthood* to the question of the major factor in what is often referred to as the parents' revolt; it also presents data for a more thorough appreciation of the content of feminism during its formative years.

CHAPTER 2

The Rights of Woman Discussion

IT has become commonplace to date modern feminism from the publication of Mary Wollstonecraft's *Vindication of the Rights of Women* in 1792,[1] although it is extremely doubtful whether the claim can be substantiated. It is true that at the time of its appearance the book caused something of a stir, but nothing like a true debate was started in the journals of the time and no books appeared to support or refute its arguments.[2] Hence in spite of its being translated into French and German and in spite of its bringing a certain fame to Mary herself, like so many of the revolutionary works of the time it was soon forgotten. A couple of pamphlets appeared in 1799[3]— and an echo reverberated from time to time as when the *Anti-Jacobin Review* lashed out at the exhortation to

'. . . bashful womankind to quit
All foolish modesty and coy grimaces'[4]

or when Shelley cried 'Can man be free if woman be a slave?'[5] —but the memory of Mary Wollstonecraft was more and more neglected; 'while the movement to which she had given perhaps the first conscious expression, was taking its first timid steps towards general recognition.'[6]

1. J. Langdon-Davis, *A Short History of Women*, revised and abridged edition, Watts, 1938, pp. 231 and 244. R. Strachey, *The Cause: a Short History of the Women's Movement in Great Britain*, Bell, London, 1928, p. 12. J. Dunbar, *The Early Victorian Woman*, Harrap, London, 1953, p. 169.
2. W. Godwin, *Memoirs of the Author of a Vindication of the Rights of Woman*, 1798, p. 81. W. C. Durant, *Supplement* to Godwin's *Memoirs of Mary Wollstonecraft*, 1927, pp. 215–19. C. K. Paul, *William Godwin: his Friends and Contemporaries*, 1867, Vol. 1, p. 205, and E. Rauschenbusch-Clough, *A Study of Mary Wollstonecraft and the Rights of Woman*, 1898, pp. 40–2.
3. See Appendix, 'List of Relevant Books and Pamphlets on the Woman Question, published in Britain in the period 1792 to 1880' below pp. 135–40.
4. 'The Vision of Liberty', August, 1801, quoted in A. E. Rodway, ed., *Godwin and the Age of Transition*, 1952, p. 218.
5. P. B. Shelley, *The Revolt of Islam*, 18, Canto Second, Stanza 43.
6. E. Rauschenbusch-Clough, *op. cit.*, p. 17.

Hence, unlike the debate which followed the publication of the *Essay on Population* in 1798 and which took the form of a controversy over the effect of population growth on a rationally planned society, Mary Wollstonecraft's little treatise on the role and status of women was ignored; and in all the mass of books and pamphlets on the population question which appeared during the next eighty years, very few indeed considered the question from the point of view of the burden of child-bearing and child-caring.[7] This must not be taken to imply that the *Vindication* was itself a contribution to the population question. The book was largely a plea for equality in education and a protest against the argument of Rousseau that woman is and should be a plaything of man.[8] Given this fact, the only way a woman can rise in the world is by marriage.

And this desire making mere animals of them, when they marry they act as such children may be expected to act—they dress, they paint, and nickname God's creatures—Surely these weak beings are only fit for a seraglio!—Can they govern a family or take care of the poor babes whom they bring into the world?[9]

Nowhere in the book does Wollstonecraft complain of the burdens the wife and mother has to carry in the fulfilment of her maternal duties. Rather does she argue that she would be able to carry them out more effectively if her education had fitted her for the task instead of providing her with 'accomplishments'. In places she obviously believes that the large family is inevitable although she does argue that if women would only suckle their children, 'they would preserve their own health, and there would be such an interval between the birth of each child, that we should seldom see a houseful of babies'.[10] On the other hand, she also argues that in order to satisfy the sexual appetites of men, many women

---

7. J. A. Banks and D. V. Glass, 'A List of Books, Pamphlets and Articles on the Population Question, published in Britain in the period 1793 to 1880' in D. V. Glass, ed., *Introduction to Malthus*, Watts, London, 1953. The list runs over 29 pages.

8. M. Wollstonecraft, *A Vindication of the Rights of Woman, with Strictures on Political and Moral Subjects*, London, 1792, Ch. 5. In this chapter she also attacks Dr. Fordyce's sermons, Dr. Gregory's *Legacy to his Daughters* and Lord Chesterfield's *Letters*.

9. *Ibid.*, Introduction, p. 9.

10. *Ibid.*, p. 443. See also pp. 99–100.

are made systematically voluptuous . . . (and) becoming, consequently, weaker, in mind and body, than they ought to be, were one
of the grand ends of their being taken into account, that of bearing
and nursing children, have not sufficient strength to discharge the
first duty of a mother; and sacrificing to lasciviousness the parental
affection, that ennobles instinct, either destroy the embryo in the
womb, or cast it off when born.[11]

Thus promiscuity 'produces a most destructive barrenness and
contagious flagitiousness of manners' and 'has an equally fatal
effect on populations and morals'. 'Surely nature never intended
that women, by satisfying an appetite, should frustrate the
very purpose for which it was implanted.'[12] There is indeed
much to be said for the view that the *Vindication of the Rights
of Woman* 'has the aim of making women better mothers' and
its analysis of the features of English culture which prevented
this took the form of a rambling sociological study rather
than a discussion of *rights* as such.[13]

To some extent this deficiency was repaired thirty years
later when William Thompson issued his *Appeal of One Half
of the Human Race* which was largely an elaborate argument for
female suffrage, on the grounds that any claim for the vote
which is based on human rights, must automatically include
women in its classes of persons for whom the claim is applicable,
and that the arguments against the inclusion of women can all
be shown to be invalid.[14] According to Macaulay the question
of votes for women had 'often been asked in parliamentary
debate' without ever receiving 'a plausible answer'[15] and there
is certainly evidence that the question was exercising people's
minds in the second decade of the nineteenth century, as utili-
tarianism gained increasing attention. Bentham was in favour
of female suffrage,[16] even if he was prepared to forgo it in the

---

11. *Ibid.*, p. 316.
12. *Ibid.*, p. 317.
13. E. Rauschenbusch-Clough, *op. cit.*, p. 157.
14. W. Thompson, *Appeal of One Half of the Human Race, Women, against
the Pretensions of the Other Half, Men, to Retain Them in Political, and Thence
in Civil and Domestic Slavery*, London, 1825.
15. T. B. Macaulay, 'Mill on Government' in the *Edinburgh Review*,
March, 1829, Vol. 49, No. 97, art. 7, p. 177.
16. J. Bentham, *Plan of Parliamentary Reform* 1817, Section 8, para. 2, in
O. Baumgardt, *Bentham and the Ethics of Today, with Bentham Manuscripts
hitherto unpublished*, Princeton University Press, New Jersey, 1952, pp.
466–8.

conditions of his time,[17] as was Shelley.[18] The 'younger prose-lytes' in Bentham's circle—John Stuart Mill and all those who formed his 'chosen associates'[19]—were in favour of it and so was even James Mill himself, in spite of some evidence to the con-trary in his *Article on Government*, if Thompson is any guide.[20]

Thompson himself, in addition to contributing to the general political argument,[21] carried the claim for enfranchisement a stage further by attempting to show that the only way in which civil and domestic rights could be assured to women would be to give them legal and political equality with men.[22]

Is there in the nature of things any security for equality of enjoy-ments, proportioned to exertion and capabilities, but by means of equal civil rights? or any security for civil rights but by means of equal political rights?

In all this Thompson displays a depth of sociological under-standing rare for his age, as for example, where he points at the difficulties facing any husband who attempts to impart 'equal happiness to his wife with that which he enjoys, or has the power of enjoying'. He is restrained by the laws and by legal and social facts working on her. 'By superstition and public opinion all her actions and enjoyments are a thousand-fold more restrained than his.'[23] The upshot is that the total effect of social, political and legal pressures is to create a slave-like mentality on the part of women who become 'confined, like other domestic animals, to the house and its little details ... The dull routine of domestic incidents is the world to them'; and deprived of knowledge and skill, excluded from 'the bene-fit of all judgment and mind-creating offices and trusts'

17. J. Bentham, *Constitutional Code*, I, Ch. 15, section 7, *Radical Reform Bill*, Section 3, art. 4, in Baumgardt, *op. cit.*, pp. 466–8.

18. P. B. Shelley, *A Philosophical View of Reform*, written 1819–20 and printed in R. J. White, ed., *Political Tracts of Wordsworth, Coleridge and Shelley*, Cambridge University Press, 1953, see p. 251.

19. J. S. Mill, *Autobiography*, 1873, Ch. 4, World's Classics ed., Oxford University Press, 1924, pp. 87–8.

20. W. Thompson, *op. cit.* Introductory Letter to Mrs. Wheeler, p. viii.

21. Thompson, *op. cit.*, pp. 18–19 and Part II, questions 1 and 2.

22. For a summary see R. K. P. Pankhurst, *William Thompson (1775–1833), Britain's Pioneer Socialist, Feminist, and Co-operator*, Watts, London, 1954, Ch. 9, and R. Saywell, *The Development of the Feminist Idea in England, 1789–1833*, unpublished M.A. thesis, London University, 1936.

23. *Ibid.*, pp. 89–91.

cut off almost entirely 'from the participation, by succession or otherwise, of property, and from its uses and exchanges' they accept the terms of the marriage 'contract' because they must.[24]

It is of some interest, in view of the later development of feminist ideas by women, that William Thompson unlike Mary Wollstonecraft did not value domestic virtues at all highly. He wrote:

> Home, except on a few occasions, chiefly for the drillings of a superstition to render her obedience more submissive, is the eternal prison-house of the wife: the husband paints it as the abode of calm bliss, but takes care to find, outside of doors, for his own use, a species of bliss not quite so calm, but of a more varied and stimulating description. These are facts of such daily occurrence and notoriety, that to the multitudinous, unreflecting, creatures, their victims, they pass by as the established order of nature. The house is *his* house with everything in it; and of all fixtures the most abjectly his is his breeding machine, the wife.[25]

It is also clear that while Thompson did not despise the rearing of children he certainly did not regard it in the same light as Mary Wollstonecraft. Children were necessary but they were not all important. They should never, for example, be allowed to interfere with more socially useful functions; and should women freely participate in political activities with men, it must be fully understood that those of them who from age were 'liable to such casualties' as child-birth, 'would always have it in their power, if any strong motive demanded it, to prevent their occurrence.'[26] Thompson was determined to end the hypocrisy surrounding sexual questions. He was scathing in his attack on the double standard of sex morality—the standard whereby 'all the evil of a vice or a crime can be made to fall on the woman, and the enjoyment can be reserved for the man'. He was equally scathing about the double standard of physical morality whereby menstruation and pregnancy were regarded as subjects for amusement.

When a man's frame is deranged by a disease brought on by his own pernicious folly, and is thus incapacitated from attending to

24. *Ibid.*, pp. 39, 55–8.
25. Thompson, *op. cit.*, pp. 79 and 85. Italics in the original.
26. *Ibid.*, pp. 35 and 78.

the most important affairs, he is pitied, and those are esteemed very unreasonable who do not accept his illness as a sufficient excuse for the neglect of their business, though ever so important. But if a woman, without being even accused of any vice or folly, is incapacitated by pain, the necessary result of organization, and indispensable for the very existence of the human race, from attending for a time to duties equally important, she is *ridiculed,* and those are ridiculed who suffer their affairs to be liable to such interruption.[27]

But above all he was convinced that the bearing and rearing of children must always place women in an inferior position *vis-à-vis* men in obtaining 'opportunities of influence' and of 'attaining their ends'.

The absolute quantity of the time of confinement during life may not, on ordinary occasions, and under improved arrangements, be much: but the *tendency* to attach too great relative importance to domestic and selfish over social and sympathetic affections, to immediate over remote objects and enjoyments, must even (if not by wise and benevolent expedients counteracted) remain with the sex which is from physical causes the most confined.[28]

This made it even more important for women to engage in political activity than for men; and to ensure this Thompson had a scheme—Association, or Labour by Mutual Co-operation —in which even the children would benefit, for they would be taken for the most part from their mothers, most of whom know nothing of 'how to form the disposition of a child for the first year of its life',[29] and would be reared in the company of their peers under the superintendence of a man or woman 'intelligent in the theory and practice of physical and mental culture'.[30]

It is strictly at this point that Thompson's work enters the field of population theory, since the problem of population growth in Co-operative Communities had already been given his attention. Unlike most other Co-operators he was inclined to accept the Malthusian argument that numbers in such communities might increase more rapidly than subsistence and hence had suggested as remedy the expedient of 'gentle exercise'—'simple, reconcilable with the utmost delicacy, and demanding nothing but a mental effort from the party whom

27. *Ibid.*, pp. 142–3.
28. *Ibid.*, p. 177. Italics in the original.
29. *Ibid.*, p. 180. Thompson places as much importance on these early years as Owen or Freud.
30. *Ibid.*, p. 179.

a new birth would most inconvenience.'[31] He does not revert
to this in the *Appeal* but it is fairly clear from both books that he
felt the whole position of women in society to be bound up
with this question, and the population question to be likewise
bound up with the question of the status of women. Men enjoyed only the pleasures of sexual union. Women also encoun-
tered the pains. In a free and equal society women might
be expected to show greater prudential foresight and thus with
the emancipation of women the problem of population pressure
would disappear.[32]

It has, however, already been shown elsewhere that such ideas
were far from popular at the time. Although the utilitarians,
Place and Carlile, made some attempt to get a birth-control
movement started, their ideas met with strong resistance.
Place's offer, indeed, to prepare tracts for working people
(on other subjects than population) was rejected by the committee of the Society for Promoting Useful Knowledge in 1834
on the ground that 'they ought to recollect what Mr. Place
had written respecting Population and to take care not to
identify the Society with him';[33] and the subject of population
limitation by physical means was *inter Christianos non nominanda*
for the next twenty years.[34] In these circumstances it is under-
standable that Thompson's work was ignored by the orthodox
Press even if it was well received in Socialist and Co-operative
circles,[35] and the subject of the relationship between the status
of women and the population question was not revived until
John Stuart Mill published his *Principles of Economics* in 1848.
In the meantime, however, the advocates of 'woman's place'

31. W. Thompson, *An Inquiry into the Principles of the Distribution of Wealth most conducive to Happiness*, 1829, pp. 547–9. These pages were omitted from Pare's abridged edition, 1850, possibly because the editor thought them unnecessary, since he rejected the Malthusian argument altogether, see his
letter in *The Political Economist*, No. 5, July, 1856.

32. W. Thompson, *Practical Directions for the Speedy and Economical Establishment of Communities, on the Principles of Mutual Co-operation, United Possessions and Equality of Exertions and of the Means of Enjoyment*, Cork, 1830, p. 232,
see Pankhurst, *op. cit.*, p. 64.

33. Quoted in J. A. Field, *op. cit.*, p. 112.

34. J. A. Banks, *Prosperity and Parenthood*, pp. 24–9.

35. Pankhurst, *op. cit.*, p. 95. See, for example, the ideal community
described in R. Cooper, *A Contrast between the New Moral World and the Old
Immoral World*, Hulme, 1838, pp. 7–10.

in the home' seem to have gathered strength. This is not to suggest that writers on this subject had not appeared before. Thomas Gisborne had devoted a book to it in 1797[36] and Gregory's *Legacy of a Father to his Daughter* was reprinted eight times between 1793 and 1838. In the 1830's and 1840's however, a whole host of new writers appeared on the scene, many of them women, and they sought to affirm the theory that it was woman's duty

> to raise herself, by every means, in the esteem of her husband . . . and thus, far more than by insisting upon her own way, or urging her own claims, she will secure a voice in her husband's counsels, and a place in his tenderest consideration.[37]

At bottom such arguments had two sources, one deriving from the biological differences between the sexes, and the other from the claims of revealed religion. The former was simplicity itself. Completely ignoring the kind of sociological analyses made by Mary Wollstonecraft and William Thompson, who tried to explain the difference between the sexes in terms of differences in their upbringing, writers like Alexander Walker believed that they were going to the root of the matter if they based themselves firmly in physiological fact and the social consequences that *necessarily* flowed from it.

> It is evident that the man, possessing reasoning faculties, muscular power, and courage to employ it, is qualified for being a protector: the woman, being little capable of reasoning, feeble, and timid, requires protection. Under such circumstances, the man naturally governs: the woman as naturally obeys.[38]

The moral was obvious:

> It would be just as rational to contend for man's right to bear children, as it is to argue for woman's participation in philosophy or legislation.[39]

The argument from nature was also used by some religious writers who professed to see in the biological differences between the sexes the evidence for the supernatural intention that women should be the helpmeet of men; but strictly speaking such an

---

36. T. Gisborne, *An Inquiry into the Duties of the Female Sex*, 1797.
37. E. Sandford, *Female Improvement*, London, 1836, Vol. 2, p. 202.
38. A. Walker, *Woman Physiologically Considered as to Mind, Morals, Marriage, Matrimonial Slavery, Infidelity and Divorce*, 2nd edition, 1840, p. 129.
39. *Ibid.*, p. 43.

elaboration was unnecessary and the more fundamentalist Christian polemic of the period was able to justify the social inferiority of women on the simple basis of the Genesis story of the creation of Eve from the rib of Adam. According to this view, woman's position in the world was necessarily inferior to that of man because it was part of the order of divine providence that it should be, and resignation to her lot was the only recourse of a woman with true Christian humility.

> Her part is to make sacrifices, in order that his enjoyment may be enhanced. [40]

And she should learn

> that the humblest occupation, undertaken from a sense of duty, becomes ennobled in the motive by which it is prompted, and that the severest self-denial may be blessed and honoured by the Father of mercies, if endured in preference to an infringement upon those laws which he has laid down for the government of the human family.[41]

It should not, however, be assumed that a full-scale controversy over the rights of women developed during this period. There was perhaps

> a breath of change in the air which called forth just at this time a definite statement of the whole position. It was as if it were felt necessary to put into words and to teach in the most deliberate manner the duty of female submissiveness which before had been taken entirely for granted.[42]

Nothing, however, in the nature of the claim and denial which characterizes the true debate, marked the literature of the day. Indeed, the next thirty years witnessed little change in this respect, at least in so far as our main theme is concerned. In the 1850's, it is true, the 'ladylike attempt' to extend the scope of education for women led to some contention about the wisdom of teaching girls the same subjects as boys;[43] in the 1860's the activities of a small group of feminists to widen the field of employment for spinsters and widows brought about some

40. S. Ellis, *The Women of England, Their Social Duties and Domestic Habits*, 1839, p. 223.

41. *Ibid.*, p. 350.

42. R. Strachey, *op. cit.*, p. 46.

43. A. C. Percival, *The English Miss, Today and Yesterday*, 1939, Chs. 5 and 6.

dispute as to the effect this might have on the economic status of wives; and in the 1870's the effort to obtain the vote for women aroused some public concern about the future of the husband's role as head of the family;[44] but nowhere in all this is there the slightest hint that a new moral code had arrived, eagerly championed by wives in revolt against the reproductive urge of the Victorian paterfamilias. A few no doubt there were whose views on the ethics of birth-control foreshadowed the outlook of the twentieth-century married woman; but they remained a relatively silent minority in the great hush surrounding the topic at this time. As compared with the emphasis on prudence and forethought in the debates on the cost of marriage,[45] there was almost nothing said on the rights of women with respect to 'the last familiarity' and the husband's power to 'enforce the lowest degradation of a human being, that of being made the instrument of an animal function contrary to her inclinations'.[46] The financial cost of children *may* have been a factor in the trend towards the smaller family, but in so far as public discussion may be our guide, a growing consideration for the discomfort, pain and dangers faced by the mother certainly was not.

In this respect the writings of John Stuart Mill stand out as an exception. Alone amongst those prominent in the feminist movement he specifically linked the rights of women with the question of population and argued that 'amongst the probable consequences of the industrial and social independence of women ... (was) ... a great diminution of the evil of over-population'.[47] It was, he added

by devoting one-half of the human species to that exclusive function, by making it fill the entire life of one sex, and interweave itself with almost all the objects of the other, that the animal instinct in question is nursed into the disproportionate preponderance which it has hitherto exercised in human life.[48]

44. R. Fulford, *Votes for Women*, 1957, Chs. 6–8.
45. J. A. Banks, *op. cit.*, Ch. 3.
46. J. S. Mill, *The Subjection of Women*, Coit's edition, 1909, p. 59.
47. J. S. Mill, *Principles of Political Economy*, Book IV, Ch. 7, § 3. This is the wording of the 3rd (1852) edition. The first edition is slightly different. For the influence of Harriet Taylor's thinking on John Stuart Mill at this time, see F. A. Hayek, *John Stuart Mill and Harriet Taylor*, 1951, Ch. 6.
48. J. S. Mill, *Principles of Political Economy, ibid.*

He did not openly advocate birth-control as the remedy, either in the *Principles of Political Economy* or in the *Subjection of Women*, although in his youth he had been arrested for distributing Francis Place's broadsheets giving advice on birth-control techniques,[49] but this may have been for purely personal reasons rather than because he had changed his mind.

As matters stood, his relations with Mrs. Taylor were the subject of gossip, and were very much misunderstood even by members of his family and by rather intimate friends. Had he been a public advocate of birth-control, what extraordinary evidence would have been lent to the accusations already afloat![50]

In any case, there was no real awakening of birth-control *propaganda* until the 1860's and then largely among the readers of the *National Reformer*.[51] This post-dated the actual writing of the *Subjection of Women*, which developed out of an article in the *Westminster Review*, although it was not published until 1869.[52]

Unlike Thompson's *Appeal*, Mill's *Subjection of Women*, was not ignored by contemporary opinion, although it probably earned him more antagonism than anything else he wrote.[53] Nevertheless the controvery it aroused did not centre upon his views on population, well known though these were. Rather was he attacked for his general theory of the nature of the distinctions between men and women, which in common with Thompson he regarded as being wholly socially determined. Such a theory ran counter to the accepted belief that the position of women in society was a product of their physical constitution or was divinely appointed. Only a minority was prepared to follow Mill, and the writings of Mrs. Sandford and Mrs. Ellis more faithfully mirror the thought of the men and women of the time than do the arguments of the handful of reformers.

The rights of women discussion, then, never entered into the main stream of controversy in the way that the population

49. M. St. J. Packe, *The Life of John Stuart Mill*, 1954, p. 57.
50. N. E. Himes, 'John Stuart Mill's Attitude toward Neo-Malthusianism', *The Economic Journal, Economic History Series*, No. 4, January, 1929, p. 481.
51. Banks, *op. cit.*, pp. 149–50. Banks and Glass, *op. cit.*, section 8.
52. Packe, *op. cit.*, p. 370.
53. Packe, *op. cit.*, pp. 495–6.

question did. Not until *after* the middle classes had begun to practise family limitation can there be said to have developed any sustained argument about an alternative 'way of life' for the married woman. The statement that

> the superintendence of a household, even when not in other respects laborious, is extremely onerous to the thoughts; it requires incessant vigilance, an eye which no detail escapes, and presents questions for consideration and solution, foreseen and unforeseen, at every hour of the day, from which the person responsible for them can hardly ever shake herself free,[54]

coming as it does from a champion of women's rights, seems to suggest that not until her domestic duties were lightened could a wife and mother extend her horizon beyond the home, and there is no evidence, from the literature of the discussion itself, that this was happening to any extent in the 1860's and 1870's.

It would nevertheless be an error to assume that because there was no discussion of the rights of women to control their own fertility there was, therefore, no relationship between the movement to change the position of women in society and the parents' revolt. Much of the organized movement for the emancipation of women concerned itself with what people considered to be particular abuses—the withholding of the franchise, for example, or the sex barriers in education. Some of these endeavours were rewarded by changes in the *status quo*—by legislation with respect of property ownership, by granting admission to the universities, by the opening up of certain professional careers to women of talent. There remains to consider therefore the possibility that the amelioration of the lot of women in these respects resulted in changes in contemporary opinion as to her role in the bearing and rearing of children, and it is to a consideration of the emancipation of women in these terms that we must now turn.

54. J. S. Mill, *Subjection of Women*, p. 101.

CHAPTER 3

The Scope of Reform

ALTHOUGH it would be a mistake to suppose that there had been no organized efforts before 1850 to reform certain aspects of woman's position in society, it was not until the middle years of the century that the sporadic and largely isolated attempts of individual reformers showed consistent evidence of becoming welded into an organized movement. Before this time there was nothing which would entitle us legitimately to speak of the woman's question or of feminism as recognizable social phenomena, and indeed it is the rapid growth in the number and importance of the attempts to improve the status of women between 1850 and 1870, which lends plausibility to the view that feminism was a causal factor in the decline in middle-class fertility which began soon afterwards. Yet, the most remarkable feature of these attempts was their outstanding lack of interest in the position of the wife and mother in a stable family relationship, and there can be little cause to doubt that the reason for this oversight was the overwhelming concern of the middle classes about the fate of their single women.

The facts which worried them may be briefly stated. In Great Britain in 1851 there were 2,765,000 single women aged 15 and over. By 1861 this figure had risen to 2,956,000 and by 1871 to 3,228,700—an increase of 16·8 per cent over the twenty years.[1] It is true that this increase was less than that for the population as a whole, or even for the age-group, 15 and over,[2] but it was the absolute numbers which bothered the Victorians, especially as these figures contained an increase of from 72,500 to 125,200 *surplus* single women, or 72·7 per cent over the twenty

---

1. Figures calculated from Table IX of *Papers of the Royal Commission on Population*, Vol. 2, *Reports and Selected Papers of the Statistics Committee*, H.M.S.O., London, 1950, pp. 202–3.
2. 25·2 per cent and 23·9 per cent respectively. *Ibid.*, Table I, p. 189.

years.[3] Some observers, moreover, believed that the growth was greater amongst the more privileged levels of society than amongst the less.

There are hundreds of thousands of women—not to speak more largely still—scattered through the ranks, but proportionately most numerous in the middle and upper classes: who have to earn their own living, instead of spending and husbanding the earnings of men; who, not having the natural duties and labour of wives and mothers, have to carve out artificial and painfully-sought occupations for themselves; who, in place of completing, sweetening, and embellishing the existence of others, are compelled to lead an independent and incomplete existence of their own. . . .[4]

Part of the explanation for this inordinate growth in the numbers of single girls who could not find husbands was no doubt the effect of the different mortality rates of the two sexes. Already by 1841 the expectation of life at birth was 40·19 years for the males of England and Wales, but 42·18 years for females.[5] During the next thirty years or so the mortality rates for both men and women declined, but more rapidly for the latter.[6] Hence, although more boy babies were born than girl babies, by the time they had reached the age of 15, diseases of all kinds and violent deaths had done much to redress the balance and turn the scale the other way.[7] This would perhaps have been less true of the children of the middle and upper classes, but insomuch as we have no separate class data, we have no means of checking.

More noticeable to contemporaries, in any case, was the difference between the sexes with respect to emigration. Accurate figures in this field are difficult to assess but there can be no disagreement about the preponderance of single men amongst the people departing permanently from British ports. Furthermore, although the authorities differ on the absolute

---

3. *Ibid.*, Tables VIII and IX, pp. 199, 202 and 203. The figure for *all* surplus women, aged 15 and over were 549,500 and 780,400 respectively, or an increase of 42·0 per cent.

4. W. R. Greg, 'Why are Women Redundant?, the *National Review*, April, 1862.

5. D. V. Glass, *Population Policies and Movements in Europe*, Oxford, University Press, 1940, p. 14.

6. W. P. D. Logan, 'Mortality in England and Wales from 1848 to 1947', *Population Studies*, Vol. 4, No. 2, September, 1950, Table I, p. 134.

7. *Ibid.*, Tables IV and V, pp. 150–3.

numbers of migrants during these years, they are agreed that the period 1851–1861 was remarkable for a considerable expansion in the flow of emigrants from Great Britain as compared with the previous decade, while the next decade fell only slightly behind it in intensity.[8] This, again, was largely a working-class phenomenon, but about 6 per cent of the permanent migrants were middle class and of these the greater part were males. Indeed, middle-class women were less inclined to emigrate than any other group in the community. Thus, whereas 2·53 per cent of all males emigrating between 1854 and 1860 were recorded as 'Gentlemen', 'Professional Men', and 'Merchants', the figure for 'Gentlewomen' and 'Governesses' formed only 0·7 per cent of all female emigrants. The figures for 1861–70 were 6·68 per cent and 5·75 per cent respectively, and for 1871–76 13·00 per cent. and 10·93 per cent. respectively, while all women formed some 30 per cent of all migrants.[9] In spite, therefore, of the attempts to deal with the problem of the surplus of middle-class spinsters by encouraging them to emigrate, the drain away of middle-class men at a faster rate continued throughout the period under review, and the women themselves protested that this was no remedy.

The men who emigrate without wives, do so because in their own opinion they cannot afford to marry. The curious idea that the women whom they would not ask in England should run after them to persuade them would be laughable if it were not mischievous.[10]

This brings us to what appears to have been the crux of the matter—'the unwillingness of men in the upper and middle classes to contract marriage'.[11] As far as we can tell, the evidence of marriage statistics shows a trend towards earlier

8. D. V. Glass, *op. cit.*, Table I, p. 2. D. V. Glass, 'A Note on the Under-Registration of Births in Britain in the 19th Century', *Population Studies*, Vol. 5, No. 1, July 1951, Table XIV, p. 86. N. H. Carrier and J. R. Jeffery, *External Migration: a Study of the Available Statistics*, General Register Office Studies on Medical and Population Subjects, No. 6, H.M.S.O., London, 1953, Table II, p. 14.

9. Carrier and Jeffrey, *op. cit.*, Tables II and XI, pp. 14 and 57.

10. 'Redundant Women', the *Victoria Magazine*, June, 1870, p. 106.

11. Victoria Discussion Society. J. Allan's paper on 'A Protest against Women's Demand for the Privileges of Both Sexes', reported in the *Victoria Magazine*, August, 1870, p. 321

marriage in the population generally during these years.[12]
Yet, writer after writer was claiming that young middle-class
men and women were postponing the entry into matrimony,
and there are good reasons for suspecting that most of the men
in this class were not marrying until their late 'twenties and
early 'thirties.[13] As Ansell reported in 1874, the average age at
marriage between 1840 and 1870 was 29·93 years for those
clergymen, doctors, lawyers, members of the aristocracy,
merchants, bankers, manufacturers, and 'gentlemen' who
returned his questionnaire.[14] Some middle-class women would
never be able to marry while the institution of monogamy
persisted. The remainder could look forward to a longer period
of courtship or even uncourted spinsterhood than had probably
been the case in their parents' generation. The questions at
issue were: what should they do with themselves? What
occupations could they find:

without losing their position in society?[15] . . . a lady, to be such,
must be a mere lady, and nothing else. She must not work for profit,
or engage in any occupation that money can command, lest she
invade the rights of the working classes, who live by their labour. . . .[16]

But the girls of the middle classes were in a more ambiguous
position:

The daughters of professional men, whose incomes average from
£500 to £1,000 a year, cannot but feel themselves a burden and a
drag on the hard-won earnings of their fathers, they must know—if
they allow themselves to think at all—that they are a constant cause
of anxiety, and that should they not get married, there is every

---

12. D. V. Glass, 'Marriage Frequency and Economic Fluctuations in
England and Wales, 1851 to 1934', in L. Hogben, ed., *Political Arithmetic:
a Symposium of Population Studies*, Allen and Unwin, London, 1938, Ch. 6,
Table I, p. 252.

13. J. A. Banks, *Prosperity and Parenthood*, Ch. 3 and Chs. 4–6, *passim*.

14. C. Ansell, Jnr., *On the Rate of Mortality, the Number of Children to a
Marriage, the Length of a Generation, and other Statistics of Families in the Upper
and Professional Classes* (1874), p. 45.

15. Victoria Discussion Society, Paper by Miss Downing on 'Work as a
Necessity for Women' reported in the *Victoria Magazine*, January, 1872,
Vol. 18, p. 221.

16. Margaretta Greg's diary, 1853, quoted in I. Pinchbeck, *Women
Workers and the Industrial Revolution, 1750–1850*, Routledge, London, 1930.
p. 315.

probability of their being, sooner or later, obliged to enter the battle of life utterly unprepared and unfitted for the fight.[17]

One occupation was traditionally open to her. She could become a governess and help to swell the ranks of the 25,000 women already employed in that work in 1851, but the pay was poor and there is some indication that the bank failures of twenty years earlier had already overstocked the market with elderly, indigent middle-class spinsters and widows. The Governesses' Benevolent Institution, for example, founded in 1841 to provide annuities and to 'afford assistance privately and delicately to ladies in temporary distress', is recorded as having received as many as 150 applications from women over 50 for an annuity of no more than £20. Eighty-three of these applicants had no money at all and suffered all the more from having been brought up in comfort.[18] In 1859 for all types of post there were 'literally hundreds of women neither well-trained nor picked, outnumbering any demand by ninety-nine per cent.[19] It is not difficult to see why governesses were popular with English novelists about this time.[20] Some alternative clearly had to be found.

The proposed remedy of emigration was, as we have seen, hardly a remedy at all. Beginning in 1849 when the National Benevolent Emigration Society was set up 'to help unfortunate gentlewomen to go to the colonies',[21] effort after effort was made during the next fifteen years but largely without success. The difficulties facing the educated woman seeking 'useful independence or happy marriage' abroad were far too great.[22] Only the 'really accomplished governesses, who command £40 to £100 in England, and who could obtain situations in the colonies, equal in money value, and superior in social position and comfort' could be 'safely' sent out.[23] For the rest

17. Miss Downing, *op. cit.*, p. 221.
18. R. Strachey, *op. cit.*, p. 60.
19. B. R. Parkes, 'A Year's Experience in Women's Work', *Transactions of the National Association for the Promotion of Social Science*, 1860, p. 813.
20. P. Thomson, *The Victorian Heroine: a Changing Ideal, 1837–1873*, Oxford University Press, London, 1956, Ch. 2.
21. W. S. Shepperson, *British Emigration to North America*, Blackwell, Oxford, 1957, p. 124.
22. Parkes, *op. cit.*, p. 818.
23. M. S. Rye, 'On Female Emigration', *Transactions of the National Association for the Promotion of Social Science*, 1862, p. 811.

some way of maintaining themselves at home was the only answer. The Society for Promoting the Employment of Women was created to meet the need.

The story of this Society is of some importance for our theme, since it formed the kernel of the women's movement of this time. It arose originally out of a committee formed to collect petitions for the Married Women's Property Bill in 1855, which was designed to extend property rights and the power to make wills to married women. The opposition to this Bill was very strong, and it was not until 1857 that it passed its Second Reading. In the meantime a Marriage and Divorce Bill had been introduced quite independently of the earlier Bill. This new Bill became law that session and since in passing there had been incorporated in it property clauses to protect deserted or divorced wives, it soon became obvious that there was little hope for more general legislation which would cover all married women. Disappointed but not altogether daunted, some of the women who had worked for the Married Women's Property Bill turned their attentions elsewhere. They acquired a magazine, the *Englishwoman's Journal*, and decided to use it to advertise posts which would be of interest to their subscribers, starting an employment register for ladies concerned with charity who

had founded, or supported, or visited industrial schools, and small hospitals, homes for invalids, and refuges of different kinds—institutions, in fact, requiring female officers.

The result was quite unexpected.

We thought that by opening a register which should act merely among our subscribers, we might occasionally find opportunities of putting the right woman into the right place . . . If in this way we got two really good and well-trained officials placed in a month, it would compensate for the little extra trouble . . . But when the whole question started into life, the advertisements put forth by the Society appear to have raised the attention of women in all parts of the country; and as the Society and the Journal now had contiguous offices in the same house, no practical distinction could be made, and the secretaries of either were literally deluged with applications for employment . . . In this way we may certainly lay claim to have heard more of women's wants during the last year than any other people in the kingdom; and that, just because the demands were so indefinite—the ladies did not want to be governesses, they wanted to be something else, and we were to advise them. In this way I conversed with ladies of all ages and conditions with young girls of seventeen finding it necessary to start in life; with single women who found teaching unendurable as life advanced: with married ladies whose husbands were invalided or not forthcoming: with widows who had children to support: with tradesmen's daughters, and with people of condition fallen into low estate.[24]

The Society for the Employment of Women was officially begun on 7 July, 1859, and was affiliated to the National Association for the Promotion of Social Science the following December.[25] The Educated Woman's Emigration Society followed soon afterwards. From the first these two organizations encouraged

the half-educated daughters of poor professional men, and . . . the children of subordinate government officers, petty shopkeepers, and artisans generally, who have been accustomed to domestic economy at home, and on whom the want of employment often pressed heavily

to try emigration,[26] and failing this to become shop assistants, clerks, telegraphists and nurses, all fields of employment which were expanding at this time. They also tried, by their own efforts, to open up new fields, such as hair dressing and printing, and attempted albeit unsuccessfully to persuade the watchmakers' and gilders' trade unions to allow girls to become apprentices. In all this they were more concerned with artisans' daughters than with the middle-class girl but they, nevertheless, gave her far more attention than she received elsewhere, at least in so far as her employment was concerned. They also fought a continuous battle against newspapers and journals like the *Saturday Review* which claimed that they were mistaken in their purpose. In its review of the first number of their Journal, for example, it had attacked them for their emphasis on the need to train girls for employment.

The end of education is to fit its subjects for that station and those duties in which the chances are that their future life will be spent.

24. Parkes, *op. cit.*, pp. 812–3. A rather different version of the founding of the Society was published in the *Englishwoman's Review*, 15 July, 1879.
25. *Transactions*, 1860, Introduction, pp. xviii–xx.
26. Rye, *op. cit.*, Miss Rye herself founded the short-lived Female Middle-Class Emigration Society in May 1862, see J. E. Lewin, 'Female Middle-Class Emigration', *Transactions of the National Association for the Promotion of Social Science*, 1863, p. 612.

As things are, it is likely while the sexes retain their present equality, that our girls, whom it is sought to put down to the desk and the counter, will have to abandon them when they become wives and mothers . . . All the time therefore that they employ in the counting-house is so much time lost—it not only does not fit them, but positively unfits them for their future duties.[27]

Against such views the Society argued the claims not only of the women who would never marry because of the numerical inequality of the sexes but also of those who did not choose to do so. 'The want of power to earn her own livelihood makes many a girl barter soul and body for money and rank', it asserted and demanded for women the right to marry or not to marry, as they thought fit.[28] It was to ensure this freedom, as well as to protect those who were compelled to earn their own living, that the Society sought to enlarge the opportunities for employment and to raise the level of wages and conditions:

We ask for a wider field of employment, so that poor milliners, whose condition benevolent gentlemen have striven in vain to improve, under the present state of the market for their labour, may not be compelled, with wasted cheeks, and glassy eyes, to work all hours of Sunday or of week-day—or to starve. We ask but to let things find a more natural and healthy level, hoping and trusting that all women, down at least to those who now struggle honestly upon the brink of a shameful and degraded life, may gather hope, and walk with firmer footing.[29]

It is not altogether surprising, therefore, to find the *English-woman's Journal* lending its columns to the demand for the opening of more professional careers for middle-class women, and more especially of a career in medicine. Already during the Crimean War Florence Nightingale had demonstrated in the most dramatic way the value of the trained and disciplined woman nurse. The troops themselves had subscribed £9,000 to enable her to 'establish and control an institute for the training, sustenance and protection of nurses, paid and unpaid'.[30]

27. 'Review of the Englishwoman's Journal', the *Saturday Review*, 10 April, 1858.

28. The *Victoria Magazine*, July 1876—an attack on Mrs. Lynn Linton's article, 'Woman's Place in Nature and Society', which had appeared in the May issue of *Belgravia*.

29. 'The Reviewer Reviewed', the *Englishwoman's Journal*, 1 May, 1858.

30. C. Woodham-Smith, *Florence Nightingale, 1820–1910*, revised and abridged edition, Penguin Books, Harmondsworth, Ch. 11, p. 184.

Four years later, in 1860, following the success of her *Notes on Nursing*, she established a training school for nurses which aimed to raise the standard of the profession. The new nurse must establish her character in a profession which had long had a reputation for drunkenness, ignorance and immorality. She must be 'neat, lady-like, vestal, above suspicion',[31] and so her training, in addition to technical competence, was concerned to produce such traits of character as punctuality, quietness, trustworthiness, personal neatness and cleanliness.

There were many who sneered at Miss Nightingale's 'lady nurses' but the experiment was a conservative one beside the more radical demand for women doctors. Enthusiasm for this project had been fired by three lectures given by Dr. Elizabeth Blackwell on 'Medicine as a Profession for Ladies', in 1859. The lecturer herself had acquired her qualifications in America only after a long struggle, and had come to Europe to give friends there some account of the progress of the American attempt to open up the medical profession to women. Her lectures excited considerable interest and a committee was formed to further the medical education of women in England. The long struggle which followed and which reached its climax in 1876 when the names of five English women doctors were added to the Register of the General Medical Council, has often been told and need not be re-told here.[32] It came too late and affected too few to have had much importance for our present purpose.[33] but it is significant to add that the promoters of the *Englishwoman's Journal* took an active part in the struggle, and that careers for women in medicine was one of their central concerns for a time.

Yet another aspect of the feminist movement of this time—its interest in reforming the education of girls—arose directly out of the problems involved in finding alternative forms of employment for women. The standard of education of the middle-class girl, largely because of the emphasis on 'accomplishments', was indeed so low that unless something could be

31. *Ibid.*, Ch. 15, p. 269.
32. Strachey, *op. cit.*, Ch. 9. E. M. Bell, *Storming the Citadel: The Rise of the Woman Doctor*, Constable, London, 1953, Chs. 1–6.
33. By December 1880 there were only 21 Registered Women Doctors in England, see the list published in the *Englishwoman's Review*, 15 January, 1881.

done to improve it, there was little hope of expanding employment opportunities for those women who needed them. It is probable in fact that the standard was even below that of the working classes at this period. When, in 1859, Angela Burdett Coutts started a scheme to attract the daughters of the middle classes into elementary-school teaching among the poor, she found that although a large number of girls came forward, they all failed to reach the necessary educational level.[34]

One of the initial steps in the long history of the opening up of higher education to girls was taken by the Governesses' Benevolent Institution under the leadership and inspiration of F. D. Maurice. It had been realized for some time that probably the most effective way of raising the status of governesses would be to provide them with some kind of certificate of proficiency, but this idea could not be implemented until provision had been made to prepare would-be governesses for such a qualification. Queen's College, which opened in 1848 in a house next door to that of the Governesses' Benevolent Institution, was designed to meet this need although in effect it was by no means confined to governesses and from the start provided a general secondary education for middle-class girls.[35]

The Ladies' College, Bedford Square, which was founded by Mrs. Elizabeth Reid a year later, seems to have been encouraged by the initial success of Queen's College. Less orthodox than its predecessor, both in the greater part taken by women in its management and in its undenominational character, as well as in its less utilitarian inspiration, it nevertheless had the same general purpose, the raising of the level of education open to girls.[36] This was also true of the North London Collegiate School, founded by Miss Buss in 1850,[37] and Cheltenham Ladies' College, which was taken over and reformed by Miss Beale in 1858.[38]

34. A. Tropp, *The School Teachers*, Heinemann, London, 1957, pp. 23–4.
35. R. G. Grylls, *Queen's College, 1848–1948*, Routledge, London, 1948, pp. 1–4.
36. M. J. Tuke, *A History of Bedford College for Women, 1849–1937*, Oxford University Press, 1939, pp. 23–5, 29–35.
37. R. M. Scrimgeour, ed., *The North London Collegiate School, 1850–1950*, Oxford University Press, 1950, pp. 30–6. J. Kamm, *How Different from Us, a biography of Miss Buss and Miss Beale*, Bodley Head, London, 1958, pp. 41–9.
38. Kamm, *op. cit.*, pp. 51–6. A. K. Clarke, *A History of the Cheltenham Ladies' College, 1853–1953*, Faber & Faber, London, 1953, pp. 43–51.

The example of these two women who had both been pupils at Queen's College was soon followed by others, also connected with either Queen's or Bedford College; but progress at first was slow. They had to combat not only the low level of existing schools and the severe shortage of skilled teachers, but also the opposition of parents who were not interested in anything but accomplishments. It was not until the 1870's that this opposition from the general public was gradually overcome. Thus whereas only ten of the present girls' public schools were opened between 1840 and 1870, thirty-six came into being between 1871 and 1880, and thirty-four between 1881 and 1890. This contrasts markedly with the development of boys' public schools, the great expansion of which took place before 1870.[39]

The 1860's also saw moves to open the universities to women. In 1862 a committee was formed to secure the admission of women to university examinations, with Emily Davies as its secretary, and one of its first steps was to secure for girls the right for the Cambridge Local Examinations. This, however, was confined to the field of secondary education and it was not until after 1870 that women gained entry to the universities.

It can fairly be said, therefore, that a large part of feminist activity between 1850 and 1870 was taken up with topics of particular concern to the unmarried rather than the married woman. Even the movement for an improvement in the education of the middle-class girl was motivated largely, although not exclusively, by the need to provide extended employment opportunities for the 'surplus' woman. Within this narrow field the feminists had a fair measure of success. The employments open to women expanded considerably between 1851 and 1871. In commerce, public administration, medicine and education the numbers employed rose from 95,000 to 138,400, an increase of 44·9 per cent in twenty years.[40] This compares with an increase of 32·1 per cent for all employed women over the same period.[41]

39. For details see Banks, *Prosperity and Parenthood, op. cit.*, pp. 189–91, 228–30.

40. Data from C. Booth, 'Occupations of the People of the United Kingdom, 1801–1881', *Journal of the Statistical Society*, Vol. 49, Pt. II, June, 1886, Appendix A (1), England and Wales, pp. 362–5. The figures are for women and girls of all ages.

41. *Ibid.*, Table II, p. 321.

It is, however, no easy matter to ascertain how much of this relatively greater expansion should be credited to feminist propaganda. The jobs which women found easiest to enter were in new and expanding areas of employment. Their efforts to break into traditionally masculine fields, such as *professional medicine*, met with little success. Moreover, in the new areas of employment the opportunities for men apparently widened at a faster rate than for women. Thus in the four occupational fields mentioned the number of men employed expanded from 156,400 in 1851 to 262,000 in 1871, an increase of 67·5 per cent.[42] Whether or not the feminist movement would have been so successful had this expansion in lower middle-class employment generally not taken place, is fortunately a question which need not concern us here, as in no sense can this aspect of the movement be linked directly to a decline in the fertility of married women.[43]

On the other hand it would be an error to think of the feminist movement during this period as concerned exclusively with single women and widows. Part of its energies was devoted to the cause of the middle-class married woman whose marriage had broken down. Unless she was protected, like many upper-class wives, by a marriage settlement, all but her personal possessions were the property of her husband. Moreover, a marriage settlement could apply only to land and stock settled in her name at the time of her marriage and anything that she might receive afterwards was unprotected. This was particularly important in the case of a woman separated from her husband, because her earnings were still legally his.[44]

There was much agitation for legal reform in the early 1850's, in which the promoters of the *Englishwoman's Journal*, the

42. *Ibid.* The numbers of *all* men employed rose only by 23·4 per cent, p. 322.

43. O. R. McGregor, 'The Social Position of Women in England, 1850–1914: A Bibliography,' *The British Journal of Sociology*, Vol. 6, No. 1, March, 1955. 'The great expansion of non-manual occupations . . . deriving from the technological and social diversification of industrialism and satisfying its cheap labour requirements, owed little to pioneering feminists', pp. 54–5.

44. A. V. Dicey, *Lectures on the Relation between Law and Public Opinion in England during the Nineteenth Century*, 2nd edition, 1914, pp. 371–83. R. H. Graveson and F. R. Crane, eds., *A Century of Family Law*, Sweet and Maxwell, London, 1957, Chs. 6 and 10.

Law Amendment Society and the National Association for the Promotion of Social Science played a prominent part. A private member's Bill was introduced into Parliament in 1857 to amend the law as it affected married women in order to give them full rights over their own property. This measure although it aroused considerable opposition from the Attorney-General, who considered it a threat to the 'social and political institutions of the nation' passed its Second Reading in the House of Commons.[45] At this stage it was overshadowed and eventually destroyed by a Government Bill on Marriage and Divorce. Largely as a result of the efforts of Caroline Norton this Bill included clauses to protect the property of a separated or divorced wife.[46] When it became law in 1858 these clauses insured that a woman who left her husband should be secure in whatever she inherited or earned after the separation. In consequence the feminists and their allies were placed at a disadvantage. The hardest of the cases on which they had relied and which had created sympathy for their cause were remedied. With these grievances removed there were few who cared about a general reform of the law of property. Even the next instalment of reform in 1870 only safe-guarded the earnings and certain other limited possessions of the married woman, and it was not until 1882 that she came into independent ownership of her property. While, therefore, changes in the law on property gave certain small victories to the feminists between 1850 and 1870, they affected divorced and separated women rather than wives in a stable family relationship, and there is little likelihood that this aspect of the movement had any direct effect on attitudes towards family size.

There were, of course, other spheres in which the feminists were active at this time. Inspired by the successes of women in organizing charitable and educational institutions and in addressing the large audiences at the annual Congresses of the National Association for the Promotion of Social Science, a small handful of them went ahead to win recognition for the place of women in public life. Their immediate aim was the

45. Speech in the House of Commons, 14 May, 1857, *Hansard*, Vol. 145, p. 275.
46. Strachey, *op. cit.*, pp. 74–6. J. G. Perkins, *Life of Mrs. Norton*, 1909. Ch. A. Acland, *Caroline Norton*, Constable, London, 1948, pp. 195–207.

Parliamentary vote, and the return of John Stuart Mill to Parliament in 1865 seemed to give them their opportunity. To their minds they had not only abstract justice but ordinary reason on their side. Quite apart from the law relating to the property of married women, there were many other legal issues, as, for example, the law relating to seduction, in which women felt that their particular needs were overlooked.[47] To secure the vote seemed the obvious, if not, indeed, the only way to ensure that their grievances were put right.[48]

In fact, however, the attempt of John Stuart Mill in 1867 and attempts by others in later years were equally unsuccessful, so that the vote was not achieved until long after the new family size was well stabilized in the middle classes. The right to vote in municipal elections was, it is true, granted quietly in 1869, to women ratepayers, but the field of local government was too limited for the measure to have any consequences for the position of the general body of women. Moreover, they were not allowed to serve as councillors or aldermen until 1894. On the other hand, the Education Act of 1870 gave women the right to serve on School Boards as well as to elect them, but this again, although providing a small number of women with useful experience in public administration, did no more than this. The same might be said of their right to become Poor Law Guardians. The achievement of a limited degree of enfranchisement, that is to say, while it gave a few women the opportunity to widen the sphere of their voluntary activities, took the feminists nowhere towards their major goal.

If we may sum up the substance of this chapter, then, it is this. Between 1850 and 1870 there was the development of an organized movement to right women's wrongs. The most widely supported and deeply felt of these concerned the fate of those women who, whether penniless spinsters and widows or deserted and ill-used wives had

to face the world and its difficulties alone, in many cases securing for themselves an honourable maintenance by the labour of their own hands, or by the efforts of their own mental prowess.[49]

---

47. *The Social and Political Dependence of Women*, 1867, pp. 28–9.
48. See J. E. Carpenter, *The Life and Work of Mary Carpenter*, London, 1881, p. 338.
49. S. Ellis, *The Education of the Heart*, 1869, p. 13.

Indeed, with the exception of a few advanced thinkers like John Stuart Mill, and, amongst the women, Barbara Leigh Smith, the feminists were not particularly concerned with the problems of the wife and mother. 'No one', said Emily Faithfull in a paper read before the Social Science Congress in 1863, 'disputes that household management and the nurture of children are good true womanly work. No one wants to take women from homes where there are home duties to perform.'[50] Such a view was very typical of feminist thought at this time. The cry against the 'madness of large families'[51] was not heard in the ranks of the movement until the 1890's, when the new pattern of family size was already established.

50. E. Faithfull, 'The Unfit Employments in which Women are Engaged'. A Paper read at the Social Science Congress and published in the *Victoria Magazine*, November, 1863. *Transactions*, 1863, p. 767 (summarized).

51. M. Caird, 'The Defence of the So-called Wild Women', *The Nineteenth Century*, May, 1892.

CHAPTER 4

The Consequences of Reform

WHATEVER the limitations of the scope of the reformers it cannot be assumed that the actual changes in the status of women during the years between 1850 and 1870 had no effect on family size. It may be that the pattern of the smaller family was an unanticipated consequence of measures designed primarily to secure greater independence for women, and that the feminist movement can indeed be termed a causative factor in the decline in middle-class fertility even if it did not work consciously to that end. With this problem in mind it is interesting to notice that the opponents of feminism certainly saw the movement as a danger to the family, and it may be helpful at this point to examine some of the charges that were made at the time. It should be emphasized, however, that both men and women might be anti-feminist for a variety of reasons some of them more rational and more articulate than others. They might, too, approve one feminist goal while opposing another, or shift their ground from time to time. Thus public opinion was gradually won over to the provision of an improved secondary education for girls by 1870, whereas approval for women's suffrage lagged considerably behind. It would, therefore, be impossible to present a detailed, comprehensive account of the anti-feminist position, even between 1850 and 1870, within the scope of this study, fascinating as such an account would be. All that will be attempted is a review of those arguments which seem to bear most nearly on the relations between husband and wife, and on the attitude towards children.

One of the most frequent and superficially most plausible of the anti-feminist arguments was that the reforms of the feminists would make women unwilling to marry. This point of view was put very forcibly by Greg in the conclusion to his well-known article 'Why are Women Redundant?' in 1862.

> To endeavour to make women independent of men; to multiply and facilitate their employment; to enable them to earn a separate

and ample subsistence . . . to induct them generally into avocations, not only as interesting and beneficient, and therefore *appropriate*, but specially and definitely as *lucrative*; to surround single life for them with so smooth an entrance . . . that marriage shall almost come to be regarded, not as their most honourable function and especial calling, but merely as one of many ways open to them . . . would appear to be the aim and theory of many female reformers . . . Few more radical or more fatal errors, we are satisfied, philanthropy has ever made.[1]

The same point was made by the *Saturday Review*, one of the most formidable and outspoken of the women's opponents.

It is not the interest of States, and it is not therefore, true social policy, to encourage the existence, as a rule, of women who are other than entirely dependent on man as well for subsistence as for protection and love . . . Married life is a woman's profession; and to this life her training—that of dependence—is modelled. Of course by not getting a husband, or by losing him, she may find that she is without resources. All that can be said of her is, she has failed in business, and no social reform can prevent such failures.[2]

Nothing could have been more uncompromising than this harsh verdict on the unmarried woman but others, if more sympathetic, were equally convinced that the policy of the feminists would only exaggerate the problem they were trying to solve. It is not always clear, however, whether the predicted decline in marriages would be due to women's love of their new-found independence, or to man's disinclination to marry an emancipated woman. A writer in *Fraser's Magazine* argued that:

It is not in the nature of things that we should teach young women to look upon non-domestic employments as a privilege, and then expect that they will value home leisure; that we should kindle ambition, and expect them to cherish obscurity, and to give themselves cheerfully to petty household details, and the patient, laborious training of children.[3]

At other times it was argued that:

men do not like, and would not seek, to mate with an independent factor, who at any time could quit—or who at all times would be tempted to neglect—the tedious duties of training and bringing up

1. *Op. cit.*, the *National Review*, April, 1862.
2. 'Queen Bees or Working Bees?' review of a paper read by Miss Bessie Parkes to the Social Science Congress, the *Saturday Review*, 12 November, 1859.
3. 'Female Labour', *Fraser's Magazine*, March, 1860.

children and keeping the tradesman's bills, and mending the linen, for the more lucrative charms of the desk or the counter.[4]

These views were vigorously challenged by the feminists themselves. Mary Taylor, for example, scoffed at those who opposed the employment of women for such reasons as these, asking:

> Why is she not to seek, and to be helped and taught to find some lucrative employment? Because her life is not to be made too easy, lest she should be less willing for the matrimony which is already what she likes best. It is surprising how often in men's schemes for ameliorating feminine evils one meets with this contradiction. Never a philanthropist takes the subject in hand but he begins by vigorously asserting that their first wish is for marriage, and that their main happiness in life must come from their husbands and children, as if the point were doubtful. Seldom, however, does he write long without betraying the belief that they adopt this career because all others are artificially closed to them, and that if a single life is made too pleasant they will not adopt it at all.[5]

The feminists indeed were scornful of the view that women would only marry if all other alternatives were closed to them, holding this to be a most cynical view of the married state. As Frances Power Cobbe wrote:

> When we have made it *less* women's interest to marry, we shall indeed have less and fewer interested marriages, with all their train of miseries and evils, but we shall have more loving ones, more marriages founded on free choice and free affection.[6]

Men too, it was sometimes argued, would be more ready to marry if women were 'more capable'. Thus Emily Faithfull thought that many men now deterred 'by prudential considerations' would be glad to marry such a woman 'who can aid her husband in his business by looking well to the ways of her household'.[7] Certainly the feminists did not look kindly on the bogey of the strong-minded woman, especially when she was put forward as the 'primary cause of the indisposition of the men of

4. 'Queen Bees or Working Bees?', the *Saturday Review*, 12 November, 1859.
5. M. Taylor, *The First Duty of Women*, London, 1870—a series of articles reprinted from the *Victoria Magazine*, 1865–70, p. 32.
6. F. P. Cobbe, 'What Shall We Do with our Old Maids?', *Fraser's Magazine*, November, 1862.
7. E. Faithfull, 'Women and Work', a paper read to the Victoria Discussion Society and published in the *Victoria Magazine*, July, 1874.

the present day to marry'.[8] Instead they called attention to the surplus of women who would remain, even if every man in England was married.

The argument that the independence of women would lead to a decrease in marriage need not be taken very seriously today. We know, for example, that although between 1881 and 1911 people were inclined to get married at a later age than had been customary among the previous generation, the proportion of them who were still unmarried by the time they had reached the ages of 50 to 54 were hardly changed, and that after 1911 the average age at marriage began to fall.[9] We know too that the trend for women in this respect was similar to that for men.[10] Details about the marriage habits of the different social classes are more difficult to obtain, but here again it seems that throughout the period 1811 to 1911, middle-class girls were only slightly older than working-class girls when they married, the difference between them being less than 1·4 years in 1871–81 rising steadily to 1·7 years in 1906–11.[11] The claim that the rising tide of feminism was a threat to marriage cannot therefore be upheld.

Other claims of the anti-feminists must, however, be taken more seriously. It was sometimes alleged, for example, that emancipated women would make bad wives and mothers. An anonymous writer in 1867 painted the picture of 'a loveless home, a wearied fretful husband' and neglected children while 'she, the mother, rules and decides the fate of nations.'[12] This, too, was the picture drawn by Beresford Hope, who, speaking on a Woman's Disabilities Bill in the House of Commons in 1870, asked:

8. 'Women and Work', the *Victoria Magazine*, March 1878—an attack on an article in the *Standard* which appeared 'on St. Valentine's Day'. The surplus of women is stated as being 800,000.

9. Report of the Royal Commission on Population, *op. cit.*, Table XIII, p. 22.

10. Glass, 'Marriage Frequency . . .', *op. cit.*, Table I, p. 252. The relevant figures are for the ages 35–45.

11. T. H. C. Stevenson, 'The Fertility of Various Social Classes in England and Wales from the Middle of the Nineteenth Century to 1911', *Journal of the Royal Statistical Society*, Vol. 83, May, 1920, Table VI, p. 426, and comment, p. 427.

12. *A Woman's View of Woman's Rights*, 1867, pp. 11–12.

what would become, not merely of woman's influence, but of her duties at home, her care of the household, her supervision of all those duties and surroundings which make a happy home; all these matters must be neglected if we are to see women coming forward and taking part in the government of the country.[13]

We can compare this view with that of a Baillie Cochrane, who, speaking in a similar debate two years later, made the surprising, but revealing, statement that the measure under discussion, the extension of the franchise to women would 'destroy the comfort of every home in the country, and eventually undermine the Constitution itself.'[14] It was the opinion of this school of thought that, whatever aptitude a woman might be trained to develop for masculine tasks, no man could perform her duties within the home. 'Man has no aptitude for domestic duties,' argued W. Landels in 1870, 'and so long as they require to be done—that is, so long as the world lasts—women will be required to do them.'[15]

All these opponents of the feminists assumed that the married woman would ignore her duties at home for the more lucrative or more exciting field of public life. Others, however, were more subtle in their approach and prophesied not that women would necessarily neglect their homes and families, but that knowledge and experience of the world and public life would make them lose the special attributes of their sex, attitudes of tenderness, affection and domesticity, which were necessary if they were to fill adequately their role as wives and mothers.[16]

No woman can or ought to know very much of the mass of meanness and wickedness and misery that is loose in the wide world. She could not learn it without losing the bloom and freshness which it is her mission in life to preserve,[17]

argued the *Saturday Review* in a characteristic passage. This journal, indeed, went so far as to declare that:

to discourage subordination in women, to countenance their com-

13. Speech of 4 May, 1870, *Hansard*, Vol. 201, p. 227.
14. Speech of 1 May, 1872, *Hansard*, Vol. 211, p. 55.
15. W. Landels, *Woman—her position and power*, London, 1870, p. 97.
16. E. K. Karslake, speech against John Stuart Mill's amendment to the Representation of the People Bill, 20 May, 1867, *Hansard*, Vol. 187, p. 833.
17. 'Conventionalities', the *Saturday Review*, 9 December, 1865.

petition in masculine careers by way of their enfranchisement is probably among the shortest methods of barbarizing our race.[18]

These views were based partly on woman's role as mother, and therefore as the educator of the race, and partly on some curious opinions as to her essential nature.

The power of reasoning is so small in women that they need adventitious help; and if they have not the guidance and check of a religious conscience, it is useless to expect from them self-control on abstract principles. They do not calculate consequences, and they are reckless when they once give way; hence they are to be kept straight only through their affections, the religious sentiment and a well-educated moral sense.[19]

It is not surprising, therefore, if the proposals of some of the feminists were seen as endangering the institutions of marriage and the family and through them the very fabric of society itself.

Moreover, this concern was not confined to such convinced anti-feminists as the writers for the *Saturday Review*. A letter from George Eliot to Emily Davies in 1868 shows quite clearly that even those generally sympathetic to a reform of the position of women had their doubts about the process of emancipation.

There lies just that kernel of truth in the vulgar alarm of men that women should be unsexed. We can no more afford to part with that exquisite type of gentleness, tenderness, possible maternity suffusing a woman's being with affectionateness, which makes what we mean by the feminine character, than we can afford to part with the human love, the mutual subjection of soul between a man and a woman.[20]

Even amongst those active within the movement itself there were some who questioned certain of its aims. Miss Beale for example, disagreed with the policy of presenting girls for the same examination as boys.

The subjects seem to me in many respects unsuited for girls, and such an examination as the one proposed is likely to further a spirit of rivalry most undesirable. I should much regret that the desire of

18. 'The Probable Retrogression of Women', the *Saturday Review*, July 1871.

19. 'The British Mother Taking Alarm', the *Saturday Review*, 9 September, 1871.

20. 8 August, 1868, quoted in B. Stephen, *Emily Davies and Girton College*, 1927, pp. 181–2.

distinction should be made in any degree a prime motive, for we should ever remember that moral training is the end, education the means. The habits of obedience to duty, of self-restraint, which the process of acquiring knowledge induces, the humility which a thoughtful and comprehensive study of the great works in literature and science tends to produce, these we would specially cultivate in a woman, that she may wear the true woman's ornaments of a meek and quiet spirit.[21]

In general, however, the feminists and their supporters were inclined to laugh at these fears as founded on a very superficial view of woman's nature. 'It is easy to talk about unsexing women,' argued the *Pall Mall Gazette*, 'but nature has kindly made that a more difficult task than theorists generally suppose.'[22] The same point was made even more forcibly by Lady Amberley.

Have these timid people so little faith in nature, so little faith in their power to win a woman, or in her instinct to be a true wife and mother, that they must hedge this rebellious creature round so that she may have no outlet except in matrimony?[23]

This is not to suppose that the feminists were unmindful of a woman's family duties. Even Emily Davies, one of the most redoubtable of the pioneers of sex equality, admitted that 'home duties fall to the lot of almost every woman, and nothing which tends to incapacitate for the performance of them ought to be encouraged'.[24] It would seem to have been the opinion of the majority of the feminists, in the words of Frances Power Cobbe, that 'the great and paramount duties of a mother and wife once adopted, every other interest sinks, by the beneficent laws of our nature, into a subordinate place in normally constituted minds'.[25] Time and again these early feminists stressed that they did not want to remove women from the

21. From a speech in 1865, see E. Raikes, *Dorothea Beale of Cheltenham*, 1908, pp. 146–7. 'It was Miss Beale's delight to show that those who did well in examinations could also excel in domestic duties. She would tell how one successful candidate of the London examinations proved first a helpful sister, then a devoted wife and mother', p. 152.
22. Quoted in the *Englishwoman's Review*, October, 1866, 'Public Opinion on Questions Concerning Women'.
23. K. Amberley, 'The Claims of Women', the *Fortnightly Review*, January, 1871.
24. E. Davies, the *Higher Education of Women*, 1866, p. 98.
25. F. P. Cobbe, 'What shall we do with our old maids?', *Fraser's Magazine*, November, 1862.

sphere of the home. This was the view of Emily Faithful,[26] and of Bessie Parkes, who argued that 'the married household is the first constituent element in national life', and that 'the immense majority of women are, and ought to be, employed in the noble duties which go to make up the Christian household'.[27]

This is not to suggest that there were no feminists who considered a career to be compatible, under certain circumstances, with a satisfactory family life. 'Does marriage necessarily involve giving up a profession?' asked Emily Davies, and answered:

On the face of it, judging by existing facts, one would incline to the contrary view. Some of the highest names in literature and art are those of married women; many schoolmistresses are married; clergymen's wives notoriously undertake a large share of extra domestic work; and there is no evidence that in any of these cases husbands are neglected, or the children worse brought up than other people's. It seems to be forgotten that women have always been married. Marriage is not a modern discovery, offering a hitherto untrodden field of action for feminine energy. The novelty is, that, as has been said already, the old field has been invaded and taken possession of by machinery. The married ladies of former days, instead of sitting in drawing-rooms, eating the bread of idleness, got through a vast amount of household business, which their successors cannot possibly do, simply because it is not there to be done. An educated woman, of active, methodological habits, blessed with good servants, as good mistresses generally are, finds an hour a day amply sufficient for her house-keeping. Nothing is gained by spreading it out over a longer time.[28]

For the middle-class married woman to confine her housekeeping to one hour a day in the face of the large families and large houses of the period was, of course, only possible at a time when domestic servants were cheap and plentiful, and the 1860's

26. E. Faithful, 'The Unfit Employments . . .', op. cit. See also the report of a paper read by her at a meeting of the Society of Arts, the *Victoria Magazine*, June, 1871.

27. B. R. Parkes, 'In Regard to Woman's Work', the *Englishwoman's Journal*, July, 1862.

28. Davies, op. cit., pp. 109–10. See also the anonymous article, 'On the Adoption of Professional Life by Women', in the *Englishwoman's Journal*, 1 September, 1858, which argued that 'if actresses and singers have conquered the difficulty, in spite of their exacting vocation, surely the painter, the sculptor, and even the physician, might do likewise'.

in particular were years of very rapid increase both in the number of domestic servants and in the servant keeping class.[29] It was against this background therefore that a writer to the *Victoria Magazine* in 1871 could argue that superintending a house did not mean doing the work of it. 'The choosing and over-looking of two or three or four servants cannot take up much of a sensible woman's time.'[30] Even children, moreover, were not necessarily to be considered 'a bar against all advance in life' as another correspondent put it. 'A professional woman spending a short time a day in the superintendence of her nursery and enjoying the society of her children, would find in it a means of rest and refreshment.[31]

The whole issue was put very neatly in an article in the *Fortnightly Review*:

> Women who had engaged in a merely bread winning profession before marriage, would give it up or not according to the circumstances of their husband; while a profession embraced from choice would probably only be abandoned if the advent of ten or twelve children made their education a more pressing and interesting consideration. For, no doubt, when women are educated, the education, technical or literary, of a large family will actually engage the time and thought which, by an amusing fiction, ladies are now supposed to bestow on the difficult task of engaging their housemaids and ordering dinner.[32]

If married women had indeed followed the advice of these feminists, we should need to look no further for the explanation of why the size of the middle-class family fell during the 1870's and after, but in fact the number of married women in the middle classes who combined a career with the responsibilities of family life was small. Although work *before* marriage had become respectable by the 1880's and 1890's the dichotomy between work *and* marriage persisted at least until the First World War. Even where married women might have welcomed the added income from work outside the home and had ample leisure to undertake it, the forces of convention were too strong for them 'to be tempted by the meagre opportunities

29. Banks, *op. cit.*, pp. 83–4.
30. The *Victoria Magazine*, August, 1871, letter from T.
31. *Ibid.*, July 1871, letter from E. M. King.
32. H. Lawrenny, 'Custom and Sex', the *Fortnightly Review*, March, 1872.

available'.[33] Nor can it be argued that the appeal of feminism drew women out of the home for public work of an unpaid kind. Charitable effort there had always been for the 'lady' and there were many who would like to have seen it extended,[34] but the increase of leisure for the female members of the growing servant-keeping classes does not seem to have been accompanied by a proportionate rise in the numbers of those engaged in work amongst the poor.[35] The opportunities too for voluntary work of a new kind, on the School Boards, for example, remained limited until the end of the century. It is difficult, therefore, to escape the conclusion that the influence of feminism on family size in this respect was small and that the argument for the possibility that it encouraged middle-class wives and mothers to spend more time outside their homes in pursuits of a pecuniary or honorific nature has little basis in fact.

This should not be taken to imply that the growing opportunities for a middle-class woman to obtain employment might not have affected the family in other ways. The anti-feminists certainly feared that if she could become economically independent of her father, brothers or husband, there was little to restrain her from open rebellion. 'In any quarrel she might have with her husband she would be enabled to say, "I have my own property, and if you don't like me I can go and live with somebody who does".'[36] John Stuart Mill's *Subjection of Women* was particularly singled out for attack on this point. He has 'almost ostentatiously refused to notice' what the probable effect of the adoption of his principles would be upon marriage, complained the *Saturday Review*:

Have we any grounds for assuming that equal rights will necessarily lead to improved morality? If we put women in every respect

33. I. Davidoff, *The Employment of Married Women in England, 1850–1950*, unpublished M.A. thesis, University of London, 1956, p. 292–4.

34. Mrs. Jameson's lectures, *Sisters of Charity*, 1855, and *Community of Labour*, 1856, were on this theme, see Strachey, *The Cause*, pp. 89–90, and the review of the 1856 lecture in *The Economist*, 29 November, 1856.

35. Cf., for example, M. B. Simey, *Charitable Effort in Liverpool in the Nineteenth Century*, Liverpool University Press, 1951, Chs. 5 and 6. For the growth of voluntary activity amongst middle-class women in the 1890's, when servants were more difficult to get, *ibid.*, pp. 125–7.

36. G. Goldrey's speech against the Married Women's Property Bill, 10 June, 1868, *Hansard*, Vol. 192, p. 1360.

on a precise equality with men, can we resist the conclusion that divorce should become voluntary, or, at the least, very much easier? The marriage law subjects women to a certain dependence on their husbands as a price for limiting the caprice and brutality of the male animal. Any destruction of the dependence must tend to make separation in some form easier than before; and whether men or women would be the greater losers by such a change, it is undeniable that a great effect would be produced upon the morals of society.[37]

It asserted on another occasion that:

Whatever gloss may be put upon it, there is no getting rid of the fact that the cardinal principle underlying the demands which are raised for a female franchise, for the legal independence of married women, and so on, is simply that marriage shall cease to be an absolute and permanent union in the sense in which it has hitherto been understood, and that it shall be reduced to a mere commercial partnership with limited liability.[38]

Divorce had, to be sure, already been made easier. The Act of 1857 had opened up the way for the middle classes to emulate what their wealthier compatriots had been able to do since 1697.[39] But, as we have already seen, the feminists as such had been largely uninterested in the campaign which led to that Act and were equally uninterested in the amendments in the divorce law which occupied the next twenty years. Divorce proceedings, moreover, continued to press more heavily on the wife than on the husband in a case of the breakdown of marital relationships, and it was on the whole the latter rather than the former who was responsible for petitioning the Courts to dissolve the marriage until well into the twentieth century.[40] In any case, the total number of divorce petitions filed, remained at between two and three per thousand marriages throughout the period under review,[41] or less than two petitions

37. 'The Subjection of Women', the *Saturday Review*, 12 February, 1870.
38. 'A Free-Love Widow', the *Saturday Review*, 18 May, 1872.
39. O. R. McGregor, *Divorce in England: a Centenary Study*, Heinemann, London, 1957, pp. 18–19.
40. G. Rowntree and N. H. Carrier, 'The Resort to Divorce in England and Wales, 1858–1957', *Population Studies*, Vol. 11, No. 3, March, 1958, Table II, p. 201.
41. Divorce statistics from Table I of Appendix II of the *Report of the Royal Commission on Marriage and Divorce*, H.M.S.O., London, 1956, p. 355, Marriages from Vol. 2 of *Papers of the Royal Commission on Population, op. cit.*, Table II, p. 209.

per 10,000 married women, aged 15–49 years.[42] It can hardly be claimed that the feminist movement, even if it had been responsible wholly for these figures, was the cause of much family breakdown—that is, in so far as this is measurable in divorce statistics.

We are consequently forced back to consider influences of a more subtle kind. How far, for example, was it the case that the emphasis on a greater independence for young middle-class women before marriage, resulted in a change in marital relationships afterwards? Was the young wife of the early 1870's more independent in her outlook as a result of feminist propaganda and feminist reform? Was she more apt to resent her subordinate position, to question her wifely duties, and above all, to limit the size of her family?

If we could answer these questions in the affirmative we should be able to claim that the feminist movement was an indirect cause of the decline in fertility; but it must be emphasized that it is no easy task to find the factual material which will provide satisfactory answers, especially when, as in the present case, the people of the day do not appear to have been aware of the significance of the questions. The anti-feminists, for example, did not anticipate that a fall in family size would be one of the possible consequences of the feminist position, at least if we are to judge by their writing or by their public speeches. They were afraid that women would not marry, that they would neglect their children for a career outside their home, or even, in extreme cases that the system of marriage itself would break down, but not that they would deliberately limit the number of their children. Indeed the actual 'flight from maternity', when it at last occurred, seems to have taken them by surprise.

Hence, in trying to relate the 'flight from maternity' to the feminist movement we find ourselves facing the problem of a lack of evidence. Although the literature on both sides of the general issue of women's rights is voluminous, that part of it which bears directly on this problem is slight indeed. It is to be noticed, however, that from the late 1860's onwards the accusation begins to be made, not so much that feminist thinking will, if carried further, lead to a revolt against maternity,

42. Rowntree and Carrier, *op. cit.*, Table II, p. 201.

as that this revolt had already started.[43] We find, for example, the *Saturday Review* during 1868 making several references to the fact that 'society has put maternity out of fashion, and the nursery is nine times out of ten a place of punishment not of pleasure to the modern mother'.[44] An article in April of that year put the case even more strongly:

> By the sacrifice of womanliness, by the sacrifice of modesty, by flattering her wooer's base preferences before marriage, by encouraging his baser selfishness afterwards, by hunting her husband to the club and restricting her maternal energies to a couple of infants, woman has at last bought her freedom. She is no slave of her husband as her mother was, she is not buried beneath the cares of a family like her grandmother.[45]

It will be noticed that although this passage hints at a considerable revolution in marital relationships there is no suggestion that this 'freedom' has any necessary connection with the 'equality' of the feminists. Nor does the following quotation, taken from the same Journal in 1871:

> No one who studies the present temper of women can shut his eyes to the fact that there is a decided diminution among them in reverence for parents, trust in men, and desire for children. . . . It is rare to find a woman, boasting herself of advanced culture, who confesses to an instinctive love for little children, or who would condescend to any of that healthy animal delight in their possession which has always been one of the most beautiful and valuable constituents of feminine nature.[46]

This is not to suggest that no one related this new attitude amongst women to the activities of the feminists, who, by now, in the late 1860's and early 1870's were busier than ever before. An article by Mrs. E. Lynn Linton, one of the most lively and

43. The *Saturday Review*, however, in 'Seduction and Infanticide', on 20 October, 1866, referred 'those persons who are clamouring for fresh branches of female occupation . . . to the recent comments of M. Arnould, who informs us that this greed for employment makes the Frenchwoman of the middle-class equally averse from having children, and, when she has them, from taking proper care of them'.

44. E. L. Linton, 'Modern Mothers', the *Saturday Review*, 29 February, 1868, reprinted in her *The Girl of the Period and Other Essays upon Social Subjects*, 1883, p. 10. See also 'What is Woman's Work', the *Saturday Review*, 15 February, 1868.

45. 'Woman and the World', the *Saturday Review*, 21 April, 1868.

46. 'The British Mother Taking Alarm', the *Saturday Review*, 9 September, 1871.

most prolific of the anti-feminist writers of this period, and a regular contributor to the *Saturday Review*, specifically connected the two movements.

> The late remarkable outbreak of women against the restrictions under which they have hitherto lived—the Modern Revolt, as it may be called—has two meanings: the one, a noble protest against the frivolity and idleness into which they have suffered themselves to sink; the other a mad rebellion against the natural duties of their sex, and those characteristics known in the mass as womanliness . . . In the question of maternity lies the saddest part of the Modern Revolt. God alone knows what good is to come out of the strange reaction against the maternal instinct, which is so marked a social feature in America, and which is spreading rapidly here. Formerly children were desired by all women, and their coming considered a blessing rather than otherwise: now the proportion of wives who regard them as a curse is something appalling, and the annoyance or despair, with the practical expression in many cases, given to that annoyance as their number increases, is simply bewildering to those who have cherished that instinct as it used to be cherished.[47]

William Acton also, in his capacity as physician, wrote in 1875 of the practical effect of this revolt showing itself in the indisposition of wives to submit sexually to their husbands.

> During the last few years and since the rights of women have been so much insisted upon, and practically carried out by 'the strongest molds of the sex' numerous husbands have complained to me of the hardships under which they suffer being married to women who regard themselves as martyrs when called upon to fulfil the duties of wives. This spirit of insubordination has become more intolerable— as the husbands assert—since it has been backed by the opinions of John Stuart Mill.[48]

This insubordination, or 'mutiny' as the *Saturday Review* called it in 1876[49] was thus seen by some observers as part of, if not caused by, the general doctrines of the feminist movement

47. E. L. Linton, 'The Modern Revolt', in *MacMillan's Magazine*, December 1870, p. 143.
48. W. Acton, *The Functions and Disorders of the Reproductive Organs in Youth, in Adult Age, and in Advanced Life, Considered in their Physiological, Social and Psychological Relations*, 6th edition, London, 1875, pp. 142-3. Acton followed this passage with a quotation from Mill's *Subjection of Women*, which refers to the wife being obliged to 'submit to the last familiarity'; see also Acton, pp. 39 and 214-5. We are indebted to Peter Cominos for this reference and for the further note that these passages were not in the 1865 edition of Acton's book.
49. 'Emancipated Women', the *Saturday Review*, 17 June, 1876.

supported by the pen of J. S. Mill. The *Saturday Review* in 1877, in an article designed to oppose the entry of women to the universities argued that:

> The Revolt of Women is not an insurrection against any grievance the removal of which would be compatible with the maintenance of the existing relations of the sexes; it is an insurrection against the lot of woman. It has its source mainly in a hatred among the more ambitious of the sex of the domestic quiet and comparative seclusion to which the woman is consigned by her duties as a wife and mother, and in a desire to go forth and play with men in the mart and on the platform the more bustling and exciting games of life. Its effect in producing, where it strongly prevails, indifference, if not aversion to maternity has been frequently noticed.[50]

Yet these same observers were aware that this 'aversion to maternity' might be shared by women who had never read John Stuart Mill, and had no desire to join with men 'in the mart and on the platform'. The nursery, argued the *Saturday Review* 'stands sadly in the way of the free development of women; it clips her social enjoyment, it curtails her bonnet bills', and so she 'pants for perfect freedom from the cares of maternity'. By limiting the size of her family she 'has her liberty'; but 'what will she do with it? As yet, freedom means simply more slang, more jewellery, more selfish extravagance, less modesty.'[51]

Such aspirations for freedom, however, can have owed little to the feminists as such. Their propaganda by 1870 had as yet reached only a small circle of women; their reforms had affected even less. Indeed, it might fairly be argued that we are dealing here with changes in the daily lives of middle-class women which were a cause rather than a consequence of feminism. Those same social and economic forces, associated with a growing middle class and a rising standard of living, which served to aggravate the problems of the single women, were also changing the busy housewives of early Victorian England into Mrs. E. Lynn Linton's modern mothers; 'so useless in their own homes, so idle, so unthrifty, so unwilling to perform their natural domestic duties'.[52]

50. 'Women at the Universities', the *Saturday Review*, 2 June, 1877.
51. 'Woman and the World', the *Saturday Review*, 11 April, 1868.
52. E. L. Linton, *Ourselves: A Series of Essays on Women*, 2nd edition, 1870, 'Our Past and Future', p. 248.

We must, therefore, conclude that the revolt from maternity cannot be simply attributable to feminist propaganda and feminist views. It may be that there were women, like those described by Acton, who refused to 'cohabit with their husbands' after reading John Stuart Mill, and who claimed for themselves, in defiance of their husbands' wishes, the right to decide for themselves whether they would again become mothers; but it would be a mistake to assume that the great majority of women who limited the size of their families did so for such reasons. We must go on to look at other and more widespread changes in the lives of middle-class women and consider whether they had greater consequences for the fall in fertility.

CHAPTER 5

The Perfect Wife

IN an earlier chapter reference was made to the appearance in the 1830's and 1840's of a host of books, produced by both male and female writers, who professed to establish the precise place of women in society and who sought to set out in very vigorous terms the duties of the wife and mother of a family.[1] 'The sphere of Domestic Life is the sphere in which female excellence is best displayed',[2] was the general line taken by this school of thought; in the home a woman was certain of being useful; domestic comfort was 'the greatest benefit she confers upon society'.[3] In attempting to assess the changes which occurred in the position of the middle-class married woman during the second half of the nineteenth century, we cannot do better than to begin with an appreciation of her role in the family as it was seen by such writers; for they most clearly reflect what members of their class believed she ought to do and be, even if individual middle-class women did not always match precept with practice.

According to this school of thought it was fundamentally the woman's task to create a home—and such a home that would provide an environment of emotional stability for her husband and children.

Not only must the house be neat and clean, but it must be so ordered as to suit the tastes of all, as far as may be, without annoyance or offence to any. Not only must a constant system of activity be established, but peace must be preserved, or happiness will be destroyed. Not only must elegance be called in, to adorn and beautify the whole, but strict integrity must be maintained by the minutest calculation as to lawful means, and self, and self-gratification, must be made the yielding point in every disputed case. Not only must an appearance of outward order and comfort be kept up, but around every domestic scene there must be a strong wall of

1. See above, pp. 22–3, and Appendix d, below pp. 135–40.
2. *Woman as She is, and as She should be*, London, 1835, p. 271.
3. Mrs. J. Sandford, *Woman in her Social and Domestic Character*, sixth edition, London, 1839, p. 2.

confidence, which no internal suspicion can undermine, no external enemy break through.[4]

This passage provides us with the key to understand why so much emphasis was laid on the sanctity of family and home. It was a place of refuge from 'those eager pecuniary speculations' and 'that fierce conflict of wordly interests, by which men are so deeply occupied as to be in a manner compelled to stifle their best feelings'.[5] It was a sanctuary in which the husband could recover from the trials of his business life and over which his wife reigned as guardian angel.[6] Alternatively, it could be thought of as 'a walled garden' with her as its queen.[7] As Ruskin put it:

the man . . . must encounter all peril and trial; to him, therefore, must be the failure, the offence, the inevitable error; often he must be wounded, or subdued; often misled, and *always* hardened. But he guards the woman from all this; within his house, as ruled by her, unless she herself has sought it, need enter no danger, no temptation, no cause of error or offence. This is the true nature of home—it is the place of Peace; the shelter, not only from all injury, but from all terror, doubt, and division.[8]

It is this contrast between the harsh competitiveness of the outside world of industry and commerce, and the seclusion of the home which most appealed to the Victorians, and explains their emphasis on the feminine virtues of gentleness and sympathy. Women might fall short in their practice of these graces but the ideal was always kept before them in the form of a home that would be 'a bright, serene, restful, joyful nook of heaven in an unheavenly world'.[9]

The contemporary theory of woman's biological nature,

4. S. Ellis, *The Women of England*, p. 26. This passage should be read not. as exhortation by Mrs. Ellis, but as a statement of the contemporary 'philosophy' underlying the English 'science of good household management', p. 25.

5. S. Ellis, *The Daughters of England*, London, 1845, pp. 22-3.

6. This is the theme of Coventry Patmore's idealization of married love, *The Angel in the House*, 1854-6.

7. This point has been thoroughly dealt with in Ch. 13 of W. E. Houghton's *The Victorian Frame of Mind*, Oxford University Press, 1957.

8. J. Ruskin, *Sesame and Lilies*, 1865, II 'Of Queens' Gardens', para. 68. See also para 53.

9. J. B. Brown, *Young Men and Maidens: a Pastoral for the Times*, London, 1871, pp. 38-9.

combined with traditional religious teaching, reinforced this concept of the wife's essentially domestic role.[10] Her position, as the 'helpmeet' of man, was inevitably a subordinate one, and it was her task, above all, to please her husband.

With grace to bear even warmth and peevishness, she must learn and adopt his tastes, study his disposition, and submit, in short, to all his desires with that graceful compliance, which in a wife is the surest sign of a sound understanding.[11]

In the same year as Mills' *Subjection of Women* Mrs. Sewell could still argue, in a book dedicated to her husband, that:

it is a man's place to rule, and a woman's to yield. He must be held up as the head of the house, and it is her duty to bend so unmurmuringly to his wishes, that the rest of the household will follow her example, and treat him with the due respect his sex demands.[12]

Yet this did not mean that the husband for his part was freed from all obligation. He was exhorted, for example, to pass over his wife's errors with indulgence, attributing 'her follies to her weakness, her imprudence to her inadvertency'. All his care and industry should be 'employed for her welfare; all his strength and power . . . exerted for her support and protection'.[13] It was his duty to provide a comfortable maintenance for her while he lived and to take steps to ensure that she was safeguarded after his death in case he should die first.[14] There was thus a clearly defined division of labour, 'the prudent management' of the wife being as necessary as the honest toil of the husband; and while he was away from home she was exhorted to 'think on him for one moment labouring with busy hand, with anxious eye and thoughtful brow, for your

10. W. Landels, *Woman's Sphere and Work, considered in the light of scripture,* London, 1859, p. 54.
11. *Woman as She is . . .*, p. 272.
12. S. A. Sewell, *Woman and the times we live in,* second edition, Manchester, 1869, pp. 28–9.
13. T. Moore, *Marriage Customs and Modes of Courtship of the Various Nations of the Universe, with remarks on the condition of women, Penn's maxims, and counsel to the single and married,* 'The Character of a Good Husband', 2nd edition, 1820, pp. 359–60.
14. J. Maynard, *Matrimony: or, what a marriage life is, and how to make the best of it,* London, 1864, Part IV, Ch. 2, 'On the Duties of a Marriage Life', 'Duties of Husbands', 3 and 4.

support and comfort', and say, 'Does he not deserve a happy home?'[15]

The duties of the perfect wife, moreover, were not confined to her obligations to her husband. Inevitably they were widened to include her duties as a mother since this was regarded as 'the consummation of the world's joy to a true woman. She has gone through the last ordeal that is required to place her in that responsible position of life which nature demands all women should attain . . .'[16] In this position she was expected to fulfill special obligations to her children. 'No one can understand so well the wants of a child as a mother—no one is so ready to meet these wants as she; and, therefore, to none but a mother, under ordinary circumstances, should the entire charge of a child be committed.'[17] Indeed, in the eyes of many, the noblest aim of her existence was 'to generate beings who, as women, may tread the footsteps of their mothers, or, as men may excel in the higher virtues which these, to them softer and sweeter occupations, render it impossible that they themselves should attain'.[18] In infancy, it was argued, the mother was the best nurse, in childhood the best guardian and instructress.[19]

It was for this reason that 'a woman when she becomes a mother should withdraw herself from the world, and devote herself to her child'.[20] An anonymous writer in 1835 pointed out the 'impropriety' of women, when they are mothers, 'aiming at mere wordly pleasures and distinction'. Instead, 'the highest honour of a virtuous woman consists in a rational seclusion'.[21] When we find the doctrines that a woman's place was in the home pressed to so literal a conclusion it is no wonder that the claims of such early feminists as Harriet and John Stuart Mill were received with consternation and alarm.[22]

15. The Religious Tract Society, *Domestic Life; or, Hints for Daily Use*, 1841, pp. 25–6.
16. Sewell, *op. cit.*, p. 40.
17. *Woman's Worth, or Hints to Raise the Female Character*, second edition, London, 1844, p. 120.
18. Walker, *op. cit.*, p. 43.
19. Sandford, *op. cit.*, p. 221.
20. Sewell, *op. cit.*, p. 43.
21. *Woman as She is . . .*, pp. 279, 282.
22. H. and J. S. Mill, 'Enfranchisement of Women', the *Westminster and Foreign Quarterly Review*, July, 1851, expressly attacked the argument for 'the incompatibility of active life with maternity, and with the cares of a household', pp. 297–8.

It must not be supposed, however, that the wife and mother was, in consequence of these doctrines, expected to be simply a household drudge. Increasingly throughout the nineteenth century manual labour in the middle-class home became the province of domestic servants recruited from the working-classes, and by the 1850's and 1860's their mistress had become 'for ever elevated above the still-room and the kitchen'.[23] Indeed, the middle-class mother was expressly enjoined to avoid all routine domestic chores in order to devote herself to the moral development of her family.

But how can she be adequate to this if the whole attention to the personal comfort of several young children devolves upon her? If she is to make and mend their articles of dress, bear them in her arms during their period of helplessness, and exhaust herself by toils throughout the day and watchings by night, how can she have leisure to study their various shades of disposition, and adapt to each the fitting mode of discipline, as the skilful gardener suits the seed to the soil? . . . The remedy is for the mother to provide herself with competent assistance in the spheres of manual labour, that she may be enabled to become the constant directress of her children, and have leisure to be happy in their companionship. This would seem to be a rational economy.[24]

The amount of actual domestic labour which, it was believed a woman ought to perform with her own hands, was dependent upon her position in society, and, as a necessary corollary, on the number of servants she kept. While a wife should not presume to live above her rank, neither should she forget, in the words of Mrs. Ellis, 'the loss of character and influence occasioned by living below our station'. While she should always be ready and able to lend assistance herself on 'extraordinary occasions' it was necessary, in general, to observe the correct mean between 'doing too much, and too little, in domestic affairs. . . . It can never be said that the atmosphere of the kitchen is an element in which a refined and intellectual woman ought to live; though the department itself is one which no sensible woman would think it a degradation to overlook.'[25]

23. 'Cooks and Cookery', a review of seven books on the subject, the *Saturday Review*, 22 February, 1862.
24. L.M.S., 'Economy', the *British Mothers' Magazine*, April, 1855, pp. 85–7.
25. S. Ellis, *The Wives of England*, pp. 219 and 260–2, see also Mrs. Sandford, *op. cit.*, pp. 215–6.

Her true position was that of 'administratrix, mainspring, guiding star of the home'.[26]

What this implied in practice is more difficult to discover but fortunately Mrs. Beeton has provided us with a detailed description of 'how to manage house, servants, and children'.[27] Her account of the housewife's day is concerned mostly with how to pay calls, to receive visitors, and to entertain generally, but it includes certain duties of a more purely domestic character. Before breakfast she must see that the children 'have received their proper ablutions'. Her next task, after breakfast, is to make the 'round of the kitchen and other offices, to see that all are in order, and that the morning's work has been properly performed by the various domestics. The orders for the day should then be given; and any questions which the domestics desire to ask, respecting their several departments, should be answered, and any special articles they may require handed to them from the store-closet.' While this ends her own purely domestic administration, even these tasks were not required by the wealthier housewife for Mrs. Beeton adds that 'in those establishments where there is a housekeeper, it will not be necessary for the mistress, personally, to perform the above-named duties'.[28]

In the ordinary middle-class household there would, however, be no housekeeper and 'after this general superintendence of her servants, the mistress, or the mother of a young family may devote herself to the instruction of some of its younger members, or to the examination of the state of their wardrobe, leaving the latter portion of the morning for reading, or for some amusing recreation'.[29] Only where the means of the mistress 'be very circumscribed' will she be 'obliged to devote a great deal of her time to the making of her children's clothes'.[30] Luncheon was

26. Mrs. Caddy, *Household Organization*, London, 1877, p. 30.
27. I. M. Beeton, *How to Manage House and Servants and to Make the Most of Your Means*, London, 1870, and *How to Manage House, Servants, and Children, with Bills of Fare for All the Year Round*, London, 1872. Neither of these books were new. They both consisted of sections reprinted from the second edition of *The Book of Household Management*, London, 1863. Isobella Beeton died in 1865.
28. I. M. Beeton, *The Book of Household Management*, London, 1869, sections 23 and 24.
29. *Ibid.*, section 25.
30. 1863 edition, section 25. The 1869 edition (section 25) amended this passage to 'where the mistress makes her own and her children's clothes, it is necessary for her to possess a Sewing Machine . . .'

normally taken by the family at the same time and from the same joint, but not necessarily together.

The usual plan is for the lady of the house to have the joint brought to her table, and afterwards carried to the nursery. But, if circumstances are not strongly against the arrangement, the children of the house may take their dinner with the mistress. It is highly conducive to the good behaviour of children to have their principal meal in the company of their mother and other members of the family, as soon as they are able to feed themselves. Many little vulgar habits and faults of speech and manner are avoided by this companionship . . . The nurse, likewise, by this plan is released, for a short period, from the care of her little charges, and, while she enjoys her dinner with her fellow-servants, the 'waiting on nurse', a great obligation with many housemaids, is avoided.[31]

While the time taken to perform these duties would clearly vary with the efficiency of the mistress and the number of her servants it is clear that for all whose means were not, as Mrs. Beeton suggests, 'very circumscribed', it would not take up a woman's whole day, or even, in many cases, a whole morning. Indeed the following semi-humorous account of what *Punch* calls the mother's Saturday review, seems hardly more onerous, in spite of its author's attempt to make it sound so:

To examine the linen when it comes home from the wash and take care that the same is properly aired and mended before distributed to its respective owners; to take the circuit of the tradesmen, and pay all the weekly bills; to take stock of the larder, and see what is wanted in the house for the ensuing week; to make a rigorous journey of inspection round the kitchen, and examine whether the cook keeps her pots and pans in a proper state of cleanliness, and if the copper kettle is as bright as it can be made; to look into the scullery and satisfy oneself that no undue quantity of rubbish is allowed to accumulate in the sink or elsewhere; to give out clean towels and sheets and table-cloths and dusters to housemaids and servants; to count over the plate with the footman . . .; to have the parlour thoroughly cleaned, and the mahogany table properly oiled and rubbed in anticipation of the morrow's dinner; to make liberal preparation for the same . . .; to get out best bonnet for church the following day; to collect all accounts and make up house-keeping book before submitting it, properly vouched and balanced, to one's lord and master; to go into the nursery after dinner, and observe with one's own maternal eyes that the young olive-branches in the

31. 1869 edition, section 26. In this section in the 1863 edition there was no reference to the children eating with their mother.

tub have their usual scrubbing and small tooth-combing once every seven days; to drill the younger children in their catechism before kissing them, and tucking them up in bed; to see that the house is closed, and everyone between the sheets, before twelve o'clock; and to do all this in the gentlest, kindliest, most methodical, and yet dignified and matronly manner, exacting obedience, and yet winning respect from all.[32]

Indeed the modern housewife contemplating her own daily tasks, might well agree with the feminists and their sympathizers who argued that there were

few things more simple than the management of an English household . . . of the daily supervision and management required, giving orders, controlling servants, etc., an hour or two in the morning is, perhaps, the utmost that anyone can spend in such business.[33]

Yet the emancipation of the English housewife of the middle and upper classes from actual domestic labour was only possible because of a cheap and plentiful supply of servants, and it is no coincidence that this pattern of living which prohibited the mistress of a family from interfering in the 'minutia of household occupation'[34] was developed and extended at a time when servants were rapidly increasing in numbers.

No middle-class household was complete in all its functions at this time unless it employed the basic minimum of three domestics, cook, parlourmaid and housemaid, or cook, parlourmaid and nursemaid. Members of the lower middle classes, of course, could not normally afford so many, and frequently were obliged to make do with a general servant or maid-of-all work, assisted occasionally by a young girl; but as they rose up the income scale they added first a housemaid or, if there were children, a nursemaid, then a cook. Beyond this point extensions were merely variations on the basic theme. The cook was provided with a kitchen maid, and later a scullery maid. Housemaids were increased in number and the whole body of servants put in charge of a housekeeper.[35] It is not surprising, therefore, to find during this period of middle-class expansion, that whereas the number of general servants increased no faster

32. 'The Mothers' Saturday Review', *Punch*, 17 December, 1859.
33. M. Grey and E. Shirreff, *Thoughts on Self-Culture, addressed to Women*, 1850, Vol. 1, p. 61.
34. *Ibid.*, Vol. 2, p. 56.
35. Banks, *op. cit.*, pp. 76–7.

than that of house-occupiers,[36] the number of cooks, housemaids and nursemaids grew more than three times as fast and house-keepers nearly six times.[37] The greatest growth, that is to say, took place amongst the more specialized classes of domestic labour; and the middle-class housewife who aspired to a household of 'gentility' was accordingly relieved of routine work herself. In consequence, she was able to give 'that necessary touch to personal toilet and to the lay-out of the meal table'.[38] However necessary it might be for the spinster and the widow to find employment, the middle-class married woman was rapidly becoming a lady of leisure.

The consequence of this development was that increasingly the women of the middle as well as the upper classes devoted little of their time to the organization of their household and spent most of the day in 'visiting, dressing, light reading', and other activities of conspicuous leisure.[39] The non-productiveness which had for long been the hall-mark of the lady was spreading down into all but the lowest ranks of the middle class. The *Saturday Review* commented acidly in 1868:

It is strange to see into what unreasonable disrepute active house-keeping—woman's first natural duty—has fallen in England. Take a family with four or five hundred a year—and we know how small that is for 'genteel humanity' in these days—the wife who will be an active housekeeper, even with such an income will be an exception to the rule . . . the snobbish half of the middle classes holds house-wifely work degrading save in the trumpery pretentiousness of 'giving orders'. Novel-reading, fancy work, visiting, letter writing, sum up her ordinary occupations and she considers them more to the point than practical housekeeping. In fact it becomes a serious question what women think themselves sent into the world for. . . .[40]

It was indeed on this point that the feminists were most in agreement with their opponents. They, too, were critical of the frivolity of girls and young women and their ignorance of domestic affairs, and they looked to a change in the quality

---

36. c. 36 per cent, 1851–71.

37. 111·5 per cent, 110·1 per cent, 121·5 per cent and 201·9 per cent, 1851–71, respectively. Banks, *op. cit.*, pp. 83–4.

38. 'Marriage', *Englishwoman's Domestic Magazine*, March 1865.

39. J. C. Ayrton, 'A Plea for Women—by one of Themselves', the *Victoria Magazine*, December, 1869.

40. 'What is Woman's Work?', the *Saturday Review*, 15 February, 1868.

of education to provide a solution to this problem.[41] For many of them an improvement in this respect would not only provide middle-class girls with better jobs if they remained single; it might also make them better wives and mothers if they married.

> Whilst marriage is held to be the only creditable destiny for women above the poorest class, the general opinion and custom of society prevent their receiving any such training, as might fit them to form and manage healthy, moral, and happy homes; and places before them instead a life of frivolity, vulgar display, and helplessness, as what they ought to aim at.[42]

It would seem, therefore, that by the 1870's the daily round of the middle-class wife involved many activities far removed from household tasks as such. Although she remained 'administratrix, mainspring, guiding star of the home' she performed very few of the actual labours necessary for its maintenance. Nor was she withdrawn from the world into a purely domestic seclusion. It is true that her outside activities, in the great majority of cases, brought her no pecuniary reward or political notoriety, yet her morning calls, her tea and whist parties, her balls and receptions often took her out of her home. In so far as this gave woman more freedom of movement it is sometimes regarded as a phase in their emancipation but there is no evidence that their position had become any less subordinate. The man was still the head of the family whose decisions had legal as well as moral authority over all its members and whose word had the ultimate sanction of physical force. Indeed, it might even be argued that as middle-class women became less productive, as they spent their time increasingly in conspicuous leisure, they became more dependent on their husbands, whose labour in business or profession made their genteel idleness a possibility.

There remains to consider how far this new pattern of behaviour, because it marked a change in the outlook of the middle classes, and irrespective of whether it may legitimately be regarded as emancipation or not, was a causal factor in the decline of family size. Certainly, the new interests

---

41. See, for example, 'Some of the Work in which Women are Deficient', the *Englishwoman's Journal*, May, 1859.

42. M. Phillipps, 'Some of the Evils arising from the present Training and Social Position of Women, and their Remedies', *Transaction of the Society for the Promotion of Social Science*, 1871, p. 590.

and new pleasures of the middle-class wife made demands upon her which were incompatible with her personally fulfilling the duties of the nursery, but for a long time there is evidence that those mothers who could afford it had handed over the care of their small children to nursemaids. Mrs. Ellis in 1843, had criticized those women who found time for morning calls, when they had none for the nursery or the schoolroom.[43] By the 1870's the number of such women had increased. The 'richly appointed nursery' with its staff of nursemaids had become the *sine qua non* of any fashionable household and a woman was considered to have done her duty by her children if she saw that they were fed, clothed and well-supplied with toys while she followed her own enjoyment elsewhere.[44] So far, indeed, did women carry their desire for freedom from the constraints of the nursery that they resorted increasingly to the wet-nurse.[45] Some of them were genuinely unable to suckle their own infants, but there is no doubt that others, often with the approval of their doctors, acted for reasons of convenience rather than necessity.[46]

This raises the question of why family planning amongst the Victorian middle classes should not have been the next step in a simple logical sequence from the employment of nursemaid and wet-nurse. Undoubtedly there had always been women who, like Queen Victoria in 1841, wished they could be relieved from what she referred to as 'the hardship and inconvenience' of child-birth, especially if it occurred too frequently. Now that a growing number of married women had become emancipated from the traditional duties of child-rearing-why should they not go on to claim emancipation from their

43. S. Ellis, *The Mothers of England, their Influence and Responsibility*, London, 1843, p. 37.

44. See 'Poor Little Freddy', the story of a little boy who pined away and died because his mother left him to the care of nurses to go to balls, etc., the *Englishwoman's Journal*, August, 1864.

45. The *British Medical Journal*, 19 June, 1869. The Enquiry was conducted by questionnaire amongst the Fellows of the Obstetrical Society. It was undertaken by William Farr.

46. A leading article in the *British Medical Journal* for 19 January, 1861, discussed the problem at some length. See also the letter from Mrs. Baines, *British Medical Journal*, 2 February, 1861, and the paper by G. Greaves, 'Observations on Some of the Causes of Infanticide', *Transactions of the Manchester Statistical Society*, Session 1862–3.

traditional duty of childbearing, or at least from some part of it? Of course, we cannot tell whether in the period 1850–70 there might not have been a growing desire on their part to shake off a little of this burden. There is some evidence that abortions among middle-class married women became more common,[47] but on the whole such a desire could not have resulted in family planning as this was a later development. All that we can say is that the transition from the perfect wife to the perfect lady in these years predisposed middle-class wives to the acceptance of birth-control once it was acceptable *on other grounds*. It remains, therefore, to consider what these other grounds might be.

It is easy to see that if the circumstances of the perfect lady were to change in such a way as to threaten the new pattern of life to which she was now accustomed, she might be induced to adopt family planning as a defensive measure. A decline in the supply of domestic servants, for example, might have presented her with the choice between having fewer children or returning to the nursery or kitchen herself. In point of fact, however, she was never faced with such a choice during this period. There was no slackening off in the employment of servants generally, or of nursemaids in particular, until well after birth-control was firmly established. So far as we can tell, there were no changes in the circumstances of the middle classes in the 1870's and after which did not affect husband and wife equally. There were no special problems facing wives as such.

We may put this differently by asserting that there is no evidence to support the view that emancipation from the traditional pattern of domesticity for middle-class women was carried through in the teeth of opposition from their husbands. On the contrary, all the evidence we have suggests that in the transition to the perfect lady they were assisted and, if anything, encouraged by the men. This indicates that the same may well have been true of the decision to practise some form of family planning, which, far from being a revolt of wives, could have been a joint decision on the part of the married couple acting together. Indeed, in the absence of any evidence that women were successful *at this time* in achieving a greater independence in decision making and in the light of their financial depen-

47. Greaves, *op. cit.*

dence on their husbands, it might well have been the case that the resolve to adopt birth-control was determined by the man alone, and that in this, as in other matters, his wife merely acquiesced. A more plausible approach to the problem, therefore, would seem to be to consider an alternative explanation for the flight from parenthood which might also be regarded as responsible for the changes in the concept of the perfect wife. We can hardly do better at this point than to reintroduce the issue of the relationship between the middle-class standard of living and family size, which has been dealt with in detail elsewhere, and which must now be reconsidered in terms of its bearing on the position of women.

CHAPTER 6

The Spread of Gentility

THE years between 1850 and 1870 were years of unexampled prosperity for the middle ranks of English society. Although retail prices rose, incomes rose faster. Greater sums of money were spent on expensive food and drink, on housing and household requirements generally. Specialist domestic servants were employed in ever increasing numbers. Middle-class men and women dined out more frequently and gave more dinner parties at home. They spent their annual holidays at seaside resorts or even abroad. They kept a horse and carriage and employed a coachman or groom. Upper middle-class women acquired a taste for expensive dress and jewellery, for the opera and other forms of entertainment. Money was increasingly invested in the education of their children, at the newly founded public schools, and at the universities. In sum, as the members of the middle classes acquired larger incomes, they attached increasing importance to the whole paraphernalia of gentility, which they came to regard as a necessary condition for a civilized existence. Our task now is to ascertain the effect of this on their attitude towards the role of the perfect wife on the one hand, and towards the size of their families on the other.

In considering their way of life we must take into account not only their actual purchasing power, which set limits beyond which the level could not rise, but also their expanding aspirations which held up before them the standards it was desirable to achieve. Throughout the period under review the purchasing power of many members of the middle class rose, and their sense of what was appropriate to the middle class way of life rose with it.[1] Thus, although retail prices went up by no more than about 5 per cent, everywhere members of the middle classes were complaining in the 1870's that every item of expenditure had increased by 50 per cent.[2] Even allowing for an inevitable

1. J. Banks, *op. cit.*, Ch. 7.
2. *Ibid.*, pp. 65–9.

exaggeration this is still a telling illustration of the new style of living which some members of the middle classes had reached and others aspired to.

One of these aspirations, as we have seen, related to the minimal requirements of three domestic servants to complete a middle-class household in all its functions. In order to maintain the standards required of them, especially if they were trying to rise in the social scale, 'middle-class men and women were obliged to employ more expensive forms of labour in larger quantities'.[3] But the employment of such specialists presupposed that their mistresses were not going to perform those tasks which they were paid to do.[4] The middle-class employer no longer engaged in the practical side of house-keeping. This was performed, often wastefully and inefficiently by servants.[5] Instead she demonstrated, by her talents as hostess, her arrangements of little dinners and 'at homes', and her success at conspicuous consumption, the ability of her husband to maintain his wife and family in luxurious idleness.

The advocates of 'gentility' were quite clear about this. Why should a young couple be content to live on £200 a year? Of course, they could manage to keep house on that sum, but not households of gentility.

They have not the concomitants of rich silk dresses, domestic evening concerts, and an elegantly appointed table. They are simply homes where the family rough it at hard work for six days of the week, enjoying only comparative leisure on the seventh day, or on other holidays few and far between, and where their womankind are commonly too busy or too tired to heed that the afternoon toilet is not perfect, or the afternoon meals not faultlessly arranged.[6]

A writer in *St. Paul's* argued:

We have to a great extent exempted women from household and menial cares; and by doing so we have secured a degree of culture and refinement not compatible, I think, with any very active interference in domestic matters. I often wish that the wiseacres who repeat the parrot cry about the happy times when ladies cooked

---

3. *Ibid.*, p. 85.
4. See 'Some of the Work in which Women are Deficient', the *Englishwoman's Journal*, May, 1859.
5. 'The Cost of Living', the *Saturday Review*, 3 April, 1875—a commentary inspired by 'The Cost of Living', in the *Cornhill Magazine*, April, 1875.
6. 'Marriage', the *Englishwoman's Domestic Magazine*, March, 1865.

their own dinners and mended their own clothes and did their own marketing, could know something of the family life of countries where women still perform the duties I see urged so eloquently upon their attention . . . I do not dispute the fact that if you wish your women-kind to be only a superior description of upper servants, you had better seek for them in these patriarchal climes. But even the courage of a Saturday Reviewer would shrink from the idea of marrying, or living with, these 'brave housewives' . . . If the nursery, and the kitchen, and the laundry are to be considered the proper sphere for the exercise of women's energies, it is idle to imagine they can also be ideal companions for the drawing-room and the study.[7]

The burden of the argument, of course, was more than that housewives should be merely ornamental; it was that they should be capable of intellectual and cultural companionship with their husbands.

If a man of intellectual tastes and pursuits wishes his wife to care for and share in them, he must in almost every case be prepared to pay the price in the shape of servants' wages.[8]

There is no doubt that the price was paid. What is not so certain is whether this was the reason for it. John Stuart Mill, it is true, thought that 'a silent domestic revolution' had taken place in his time which had changed the relations between the sexes.

Women and men are, for the first time in history, really each others companions. Our traditions respecting the proper relations between them have descended from a time when their lives were apart—when they were separate in their thoughts, because they were separate equally in their amusements and in their serious occupations. In former days a man passed his life among men; all his friendships, all his real intimacies, were with men; with men alone did he consult on any serious business; the wife was either a plaything or an upper servant. All this, among the educated classes, is now changed. The man no longer gives his spare hours to violent outdoor exercises and boisterous conviviality with male associates; the two sexes now pass their lives together; the women of a man's family are his habitual society; the wife is his chief associate, his most confidential friend, and often his most trusted adviser.[9]

There may be some truth in this, but on the other hand,

7. *St. Paul's*, June, 1868, quoted in the *Englishwoman's Review*, July, 1868.
8. 'Luxury', the *Cornhill Magazine*, September, 1860.
9. J. S. Mill, speech in moving his amendment to the Representation of the People Bill, House of Commons, 20 May, 1867, *Hansard*, Vol. 187, p. 821.

Mill's own relations with Harriet Taylor may well have coloured his views on what was happening around him. Indeed, it may be doubted whether many wives were equipped for the kind of intellectual companionship that Mill was speaking of. It is likely that professional men would have agreed with Creighton, rather than with Mill, when the former wrote that he found:

> ladies in general very unsatisfactory mental food: they seem to have no particular thoughts or ideas, and though for a time it is flattering to one's vanity to think one may teach them some, it palls after a while. Of course at a certain age, when you have a house and so on, you get a wife as part of its furniture, and find her a very comfortable institution; but I doubt greatly whether there were ever many men who had thoughts worth recounting, who told these thoughts to their wives at first, or who expected them to appreciate them.[10]

The truth would seem to be that the men of the middle classes increasingly demanded a degree of comfort and refinement in their home-life which, whether or not it included a close intellectual companionship with their wives, was incompatible with 'a German mode of life, in which the women of the family are sometimes little better than servants and have few ideas beyond household management.'[11] Thus the middle-class housewife was not simply avoiding hard or unpleasant tasks. She was trying to meet the standards expected of people in her position.

> As her means increase every wife transfers every household duty involving labour to other hands. As soon as she is able to afford it she hires a washer-woman occasionally, then a charwoman, then a cook and housemaid, a nurse or two, a governess, a lady's maid, a housekeeper—and no blame attaches to any step of her progress, unless the payment is beyond her means.[12]

The emphasis here is quite clear; the matter was one of achieving and maintaining social status. Provided she did not try to live *above* her income, provided she remembered that 'debt wantonly incurred, without the certainty of the power of pay-

10. Letter to R. T. Raikes, 6 August, 1866, reproduced in L. Creighton, *Life and Letters of Mandell Creighton*, 1904, Vol. 1, p. 33. Creighton was twenty-three at the time.
11. 'Household Regeneration', the *Saturday Review*, 17 March, 1877—a review of Mrs. Caddy's *Household Organization*.
12. M. Taylor, *The First Duty of Women*, 1870, p. 51.

ment, is the meanest species of dishonesty'[13] there was no blame, indeed there might even be a positive duty, in living up to whatever social position her husband's means could afford.

Much the same consideration applies to another aspect of the spread of gentility, expenditure on women's dress. Cunnington has called the period from 1866 to 1880 the 'golden age' of the dressmakers' art.

Never before or since has the Englishwoman's costume been so complex, reaching a degree which defied even the professional fashion journalist to describe. In a technical sense it seems as though the costumier was indulging in sheer bravura display, inventing new difficulties in order to show her skill in overcoming them. The moment was auspicious. Materials had reached a high level of excellence. Until the wave of prosperity began to decline, late in the 'seventies, the demand for fine clothes was wider than ever and extravagance in dress had become habitual among the class represented by the Perfect Lady.[14]

A whole range of fashions was possible, requiring as many as five or six changes a day.[15] Special walking dresses and afternoon dresses came to be regarded as a necessary part of the wardrobe of the lady of fashion in the 1860's, and evening dresses of all kinds elaborated the variety and richness of their trimmings during the next twenty years.[16] The tennis-dress, that 'forerunner of a distinct style for outdoor games' did not appear, it is true, until 1877, but by that time the tailor-made costume, derived from the older riding-habit, was firmly established.[17] Throughout the 1860's and 1870's the evidence all points to a growing awareness that women's clothing had become increasingly expensive, although yard for yard the cost of raw materials fell.[18]

We may conclude, therefore, that by the 1870's the notion of the perfect wife included that of the perfect lady—leisured, elegant, and above all expensive. Indeed, since married women

13. *Home Truths for Home Peace or 'Muddle Defeated'; a practical inquiry into what chiefly mars or makes the comfort of domestic life; especially addressed to young housewives*, second edition, London, 1852, p. 137.
14. C. W. Cunnington, *The Perfect Lady*, Parrish, London, 1948, p. 39.
15. *Ibid.*, p. 40.
16. C. W. Cunnington, *English Women's Clothing in the Nineteenth Century*, Faber, London, 1937, Chs. 7 and 8, *passim*.
17. *Ibid.*, p. 283.
18. Banks, *op. cit.*, pp. 96–100.

were permitted a 'richer style of dress' it is most likely that they cost more to clothe than did the unmarried girl.[19] We are not, therefore, surprised to meet the frequent complaint that young men could not afford to marry, for they could not afford to maintain such a wife. Greg, for example, in attempting to account for the excess of unmarried women gave as one reason 'the growing and morbid luxury of the age' which encouraged women to refuse marriage in order to preserve 'that "position" which they value more than the attractions of domestic life'. The number of such women, he argued, was 'considerable' in the middle ranks of society and 'enormous' in the higher. 'To speak broadly', he went on, 'as wives become less expensive and less exigeant, more men will learn to prefer them to mistresses.'[20]

It had, indeed, become customary for young couples to expect that they should start married life at the level of living which their parents had reached, and it was accepted as right and proper that a man should not marry until he had a reasonable prospect of maintaining such a level.[21] 'No man,' it was argued, 'wishes to ask a women to take a position of less comfort than she has been accustomed to and has a right to expect; no woman wishes to be a burden to the man she loves.'[22]

The virtues of prudence and restraint were already dominant in the middle-class ethos, and a consideration of the proper time to marry was as important to the bachelor as the choice of a proper wife.[23] When considering a career, whether in medicine, the law or the Church, it was recognized that 'the money question, after all, resolves itself into the question, "when shall I marry?"'[24] and to plunge into an ill-considered early marriage was the height of folly.[25] As the standard of living rose, so did the cost of supporting a wife, and the preoccupation of the prudent bachelor with the proper time to marry grew more

19. Madame Rosalie, 'Hints for the Toilet', the *Family Friend*, May 1864.
20. Greg, 'Why Are Women Redundant', *op. cit.*, April, 1862.
21. S. A. Sewell, *Woman and the Times we live in*, second edition, Manchester, 1869, pp. 30–31. For other examples, see Banks, *op. cit.*, pp. 44–5.
22. T. L. Nichols, *Behaviour: a manual of manners and morals*, London, 1874, p. 145.
23. See the examples given in Banks, *op. cit.*, pp. 35–7, 40–7.
24. 'The Church as a Profession', the *Cornhill Magazine*, June, 1864.
25. Banks, *op. cit.*, p. 37.

intense. The age at which he could afford to marry was necessarily still further postponed, as argued the *Saturday Review* in 1875.

> The same income which enabled a middle-class family to live in comfort twenty years ago will not do so now. This is partly because of the rise in prices, but chiefly because many things which used to come under the head of the luxuries of life have now become necessities . . . Young men do not marry as early as they did fifty years ago.[26]

It was, indeed, even suggested that some men could not afford to marry at all. 'Life is so much more costly and luxurious than it was,' wrote Mrs. Lynn Linton, 'and men in consequence so much more disinclined to marry on small incomes.'[27] The dangers of so doing were graphically described by a writer in the *Medical Critic and Psychological Journal* who gave it as his opinion that:

> most medical men would be better if they remain single. We know that it is opposed to the received opinion on the subject, and we own that it has its inconveniences. But we feel confident that, in the present state of society, in which expensive luxury forms a constant element, it is next to impossible for a general practitioner to support a proper appearance in the world from nothing more than the proceeds of his professional exertions. It is the married life that urges so many to work themselves to death.[28]

It would not, of course, be true to suggest that this flight from marriage, in so far as it took place, was due solely to the expense of a wife. It was the whole cost of marriage that was involved, and this included a high standard of luxury for the whole family. It was not simply that 'the ladies must have their

26. 'Work for Women', the *Saturday Review*, 3 April, 1875.
27. E. L. Linton, *Ourselves: a Series of Essays on Women*, second edition, 1870, p. 247. See also the correspondence in *The Times*, January, 1858 and June and July, 1861, summarized in Banks, *op. cit.*, pp. 41–5. The latter correspondence is also dealt with from a slightly different point of view in C. Pear, *The Girl with the Swansdown Seat*, Muller, London, 1955, pp. 101–105. The *Daily Telegraph* ran a similar correspondence in the early part of 1868, see 'Marriage versus Celibacy', *Belgravia, a London Magazine*, August, 1868. Marie Stopes believes this correspondence to have been significant in the spread of contraceptive ideas, *Contraception*, sixth edition, Putnam, London, 1946, p. 304.
28. Quoted in 'Marriage of a Medical Man not Advisable', the *British Medical Journal*, 23 November, 1861.

splendid silks and expensive lace, or they positively affirm they
have "nothing to wear"'. The gentlemen too, 'must have their
sumptuous dinners, well served, and expensive wines, or they
raise the piteous cry they have "nothing to eat"; the family must
possess its suburban mansion, elegantly furnished, its gay
equipage, and its rounds of balls and parties, or else life becomes
a mean vulgar thing, scarcely to be endured.'[29] Wine, which in
the ranks of the middle classes had formerly been 'a luxury for
high days and holidays, is now seen daily on every table'[30] and
wine imports increased by 200 per cent per head of the population between 1858–60 and 1882–4.[31] Nor was increasing
expense

confined altogether, or even chiefly, to domestic matters. On the
contrary it pervades every condition, every object around us. The
accommodation, the fitting up, and the decorations of the shop,
offices, or counting-house, are now all after a style necessitating
the expenditure of as much capital as would, a few years back, have
purchased half a tradesman's stock-in-trade, and men say, and very
truly, that they have no chance of succeeding if they do not, in these
things, keep pace with their neighbours.[32]

All this had to be taken into account in estimating the proper
time to marry, but above all, a young man had to consider the
cost of children, for the expense of maintaining a large family
was likely to be considerable. Food and clothing had of course
to be found, although so long as children were small neither
of these was likely to be an important item. On the whole
children's food was confined to 'the strictly wholesome',[33]
and was plain and sparse, as part of the general attitude that

29. *Meliora: a Quarterly Review of Social Science*, Vol. 3, 1861, p. 105.
30. T. Markby, 'Public Schools', a review of the *Report of the Commission
on Public Schools*, 1864, and the *Public Schools Calendar*, 1866, in which he
deals with the effect of 'changes of manners', the *Contemporary Review*,
February, 1867.
31. M. Bateson, 'Social Life', Ch. 24 of D. H. Traill and J. S. Mann,
Social England, 1897.
32. 'Marriage', the *Englishwoman's Domestic Magazine*, March, 1865.
33. *Cassell's Household Guide: being a complete encyclopaedia of Domestic and
Social Economy, and Forming a Guide to Every Department of Practical Life*,
London, 1871, Vol. 1, p. 343. *Cassell's* aim was to increase the variety of
children's food. See also Banks, *op. cit.*, pp. 170–2.

children should not be 'molly-coddled'.[34] Expensive toys were quite out of the question and home dressmaking was the rule for clothing, except perhaps in the case of 'best clothes' and school uniforms which became more common in the 1860's.[35]

More costly in the long run was the increase in domestic assistance as nursemaid was added to nursemaid in order to maintain the efficiency of the nursery, but this was still only part of the expense. Room had also to be found to house the growing family with its attendant domestics.

In Bayswater and Paddington, in Bloomsbury, in Pimlico, in Brompton, in Camberwell, and in other districts too numerous to mention, there are thousands of houses which no one would live in who had not a family, and which no one who has a family can live in unless he is prepared to spend from £500 to £1,500 a year.[36]

There were other expenses, small perhaps in themselves, but which were an added burden as the family grew in size. These included 'proper medical attendance' which might, of course, involve considerable expenditure if one or other of the children were sickly, and 'an occasional change of air'.[37] The annual holiday by the sea was considered necessary for the health as well as the pleasure of both parents and children. Indeed, 'the fashion of "a change to the sea-side" every autumn has of late years prevailed to so great an extent throughout Europe, but especially England, that it has almost amounted to a mania.'[38]

It is likely that expenditure under all these headings increased in varying degrees between 1850 and 1870. Moreover, apart from the effect of rising standards children were also costing more because they were living longer. With a fall in infant- and child-death rates rather more children were surviving to adult-

34. *Enquire within Upon Everything*, 1870, item 1831, 'We learn from daily experience, that children who have been the least indulged, thrive much better . . ., etc.', p. 256. See also M. E. Perugini, *Victorian Days and Ways*, 1946, Ch. 8, pp. 89–90 and *passim*.
35. Banks, *op. cit.*, p. 172.
36. 'Luxury', the *Cornhill Magazine*, September, 1860.
37. *Ibid.* Country air and sea-bathing were regarded 'almost as necessities for our children, if we inhabit large cities', 'High Living with Low Means', the *Family Friend*, May, 1861.
38. *Cassell's Household Guide*, *op. cit.*, Vol. 2, p. 211, see also Banks, *op. cit.*, pp. 94–5. J. A. R. Pimlott, *The Englishman's Holiday, a Social History*, Faber, London, 1947, pp. 105–6, 111, 118–22.

hood.[39] This not only intensified the difficulty of feeding, clothing and housing a large and growing family, it made even more acute the problem of giving it an appropriate education. Between 1850 and 1870 three times as many public schools were founded as during a whole century previously. Middle-class parents had come to accept the idea of spending money on the education of their children, especially their sons, as an essential part of their pattern of life. Professional careers in medicine and the law were already dependent on the passing of university and other examinations, and with the extension of the examination system to the Civil Service, the importance of a formal educational background increased.[40] By 1868 a large number of the upper-middle classes, it was reported, 'are now looking forward to qualify themselves for Government appointments'.[41]

A period at the university was also advocated as a necessary mark of good breeding.

> There can, we think be no doubt that a young man in the class of which we are speaking ought to go to the University, and if possible take his degree: the former at all costs, the latter also if he is designed for a learned profession: and even in any time of life in which a man is to mix in educated society, he is all the better for having the University stamp upon him: and in no case is it more valuable than where his line of life is cast on debatable ground: that is, one which does not, in the eyes of the world, stand quite on an equality with a learned profession, and which may, therefore, give a man a certain distrust of the exact position he occupies in society . . . In an age in which many who would, some years ago, have taken to a learned profession, are now directing themselves to more lucrative occupations, we are sure that the considerations we have been urging are well worth the attention of those whom they may concern.[42]

Upper middle-class parents who were swayed by arguments

39. W. P. D. Logan, 'Mortality in England and Wales from 1848 to 1947', *Population Studies*, Vol. 4, No. 2, September 1950, pp. 133–55, Banks, *op. cit.*, pp. 194–5.

40. *Ibid.*, pp. 173–91.

41. Report of the School Inquiry Commission, *Parliamentary Papers*, 1867–8, Vol. 4, Minutes of Evidence taken before the Commissioners, Part I, evidence of W. B. Carpenter, Registrar, University of London, 14 March, 1865, question 947.

42. W. E. Jelf, 'Home and School Education', the *Contemporary Review*, October, 1866. Of course, there were critics of the trend, see 'Getting our Sons off our Hands', the *Englishwoman's Domestic Magazine*, March, 1865.

such as these would have to be prepared to meet a considerable bill for the education of their sons. By 1870 'the cost facing an upper middle-class parent with three sons to be sent to public school, Oxford or Cambridge, and then into one of the professions, an average say of eight years per son at £200 per year, was £4,800 or £267 per annum for eighteen years'.[43] The cost of educating a daughter would normally be much less, but against this must be set the greater cost of her clothes, and the fact that she had to be supported at home until she married.

Against this background of rising costs of children the middle-class bachelor doubted the wisdom of early marriages. His concern with their cost, of course, must be considered in the light of the general belief that children were inevitable and should be planned for. Granted that babies were, in Matthew Arnold's phrase, 'sent',[44] and might arrive before the marriage had lasted a year, it was perfectly reasonable to postpone the wedding until there were good prospects of supporting not only a wife but a growing family. Accordingly, a young man would be 'accepted on the understanding' that marriage would be delayed until his income was on the upward grade;[45] and for the period after 1850 such an understanding made good sense, because, with the economic expansion of the middle classes, he could anticipate a steady series of income increases in the future stretching out before him at least until middle age.

The tendency to postpone marriage, therefore, must be seen as a consequence of the spread of gentility into the middle classes. Although incomes were rising during this period it seems likely that they did not always keep pace with aspirations. Once it was accepted that a young couple should begin their married life at a level which their parents had reached only by middle age, it was impossible to regard early marriage as anything but imprudent. Moreover, since postponement of marriage was one of the factors responsible for increasing the number of 'redundant' women in the population it can be seen that the spread of gentility was itself an indirect cause of the movement

43. Banks, *op. cit.*, p. 194.
44. M. Arnold, *Culture and Anarchy: an essay in political and social criticism,* 1869, Ch. 6.
45. W. F. M. Weston-Webb, *The Autobiography of a British Yarn Merchant, 1929,* p. 78.

to find employment for those middle-class girls and women who had 'no male creatures at hand to keep them'.[46] This aspect of feminism, that is to say, was indirectly a product of the rising standard of living which was so marked a feature of middle-class existence between 1850 and 1870.

Yet, as we have seen, this was in no way a movement to alter the position of the married woman and mother. Indeed, in so far as the spread of gentility was responsible for the development of the idea that the perfect woman should be elegant and leisured, the rising standards resulted not in greater emancipation but in increased dependence upon her husband; and there is no evidence that any but a tiny fraction of wives resented this dependence. It was not yet time for Nora to leave her Doll's House. Women, as much as men, admired the 'womanly woman'. Women, as much as men shrank from the 'strong-minded female'. No doubt there were times when both men and women complained that 'helpless women are such a bore', but they could always comfort themselves with the thought that 'very independent women are not lovable'.[47] There are no signs, even in the 1870's, of the emancipation of women in the home.

It was in the 1870's, however, that the notion of family limitation first began to be widely accepted amongst the members of the upper middle classes. The propaganda of Francis Place in the 1820's had been received with repugnance and his 'To the Married of both Sexes in Genteel Life' had been ignored.[48] Then, after forty years of almost complete silence, a fresh wave of propaganda was started which, culminating in the famous Bradlaugh-Besant trial of 1877, helped to publicise the Neo-Malthusian arguments.[49] Moreover this time, and in

46. E. L. Linton, *Ourselves, op. cit.*, p. 45.
47. 'Climbing the Hill: a Story for the Household', by the Author of 'A Trap to Catch a Sunbeam', etc. *The Household: a Book of Reference upon Subjects Relating to Domestic Economy and Home Enjoyment*, 1866, p. 41. This was not so much a story as a series of domestic sketches starting with the marriage of the two main characters, an architect and a city merchant's daughter. Note that after six years of marriage they have five children, p. 362.
48. Facsimile copies of this 'diabolic handbill' are reproduced in M. Stopes, *Contraception*, Plate X, and in N. E. Himes, 'The Birth-Control Handbills of 1823', the *Lancet*, 6 August, 1927.
49. J. A. and Olive Banks, 'The Bradlaugh-Besant Trial and the English Newspapers', *Population Studies*, Vol. 8, No. 1, July, 1954.

spite of the almost hysterical opposition of sections of the press, and the bitter denunciation of the medical profession, there is evidence that sections of the public were now sympathetic to these arguments and ready to implement the notion of positive family planning, even involving recourse to contraception, as opposed to mere postponement of marriage.

Why should the upper-middle classes, so indifferent if not hostile to the idea of family planning before the 1870's, be willing to act upon it afterwards? One possible answer has already been given.

The years of the 1870's and onwards were years of some difficulty for those in receipt of middle- and upper-range incomes. Prices fell, it is true, but incomes suffered something of a set-back too. Servants' wages rose and their labour became more difficult to obtain. Hence, in comparison with the lower middle classes, the better-off sections of society were faced with a greater struggle to maintain and extend the differential standard. The years of what had promised to be inevitable progress had passed away. Some kind of personal planning was necessary now if the social hierarchy was to be preserved.[50]

The rationale is clear. Up to the 1870's the maintenance of gentility, although it frequently presupposed the postponement of marriage, 'did not require the additional notion of the control of births'. Once the young man was fully established in his business or profession, marriage was possible because although children might come at a fairly rapid rate he could always be confident that his income would rise sufficiently to cover his fresh commitments. After 1873 middle-class men and women appear to have thought differently. Their sense of security had been very seriously shaken by the Great Depression and

soon the early optimism of an earlier age died away. For such people postponement of marriage would obviously cease to have appeal for there could be no point in waiting for a prosperity which they were now convinced might never come.[51]

When we look at the flight from parenthood from this point of view it is clear that it was very far from being a revolt of women. Both sexes were concerned to maintain the standard of living to which they had become accustomed, and were ready to accept birth-control to solve their economic problems. Indeed,

50. Banks, *Prosperity and Parenthood*, p. 138.
51. *Ibid.*, p. 200.

in so far as the initiative in proposing marriage was customarily a male affair, and in so far as postponement of marriage now gave way to family planning within marriage, it is not unreasonable to argue that the initiative for birth-control came from the men. However, be that as it may, the point remains that neither feminism as such nor the emancipation of the middle-class woman from her traditional role of home-maker were important causal factors in the decline in family size. The case for the overriding significance of the standard of living is accordingly strengthened, especially as this has already been shown to have had important consequences of its own in increasing the need to find incomes for unmarried and widowed women, and hence in strengthening the feminist movement for reform, and at the same time turning the middle-class wife from an economically useful member of the household into an elegant and expensive lady of leisure.

Nevertheless, this account of feminism and family planning would not be complete without a description of the feminist attitude to the use of contraception, as it was at the time of the Bradlaugh-Besant trial and as it continued for many years after family planning was already a fact. If birth-control played no part in the general feminist platform before 1870, the question necessarily arises: when did it at last find a place? It is to this and allied questions that we now turn.

CHAPTER 7

The 1870's and After

IT has become a commonplace to refer to the 1870's as 'a watershed in English life'.[1] The establishment of a national system of elementary education, the extension of the franchise to part of the urban working class, and the legal recognition of trade unionism about this time marked a definite change in the position of the working man in society. The abolition of the system by which commissions and promotions in the army might be purchased, and the extension of entry by competitive examination to most branches of the Civil Service were equally significant for the middle classes. But above all, the practice of family limitations which was coming to be firmly established amongst, eventually, all classes has had profound repercussions on domestic life in general and on the position of women in particular.

It would, of course, be absurd to attempt to establish a precise date for a social revolution of this magnitude. Long before the 1870's family limitation had been known and practised, but we have no knowledge of its extent because of the veil of secrecy which was drawn over this aspect of life. Certainly there is evidence of some desire on the part of middle-class men and women for relief from the burden of child-bearing;[2] but the evidence is scanty and the statistics we have of births, marriages and deaths bear witness to the fact that this desire made little impact on the population of the day. The first real sign of change, indeed, made its appearance in the 1860's, not merely with the awakening of birth-control propaganda but with a protest on the part of a number of medical men that

1. R. C. K. Ensor, *England, 1870–1914*, Oxford University Press, 1936, p. 136.
2. Banks, *Prosperity and Parenthood*, pp. 142–5. Ansell, in his enquiry into the reproductive statistics of the upper and professional classes, *op. cit.*, 1874, reproduced a drawing by one of them expressing his appreciation of the fact that his wife had attained the menopause. It bears the caption 'Hurrah, there will be no more of them'.

baby-farming, infanticide and abortion were on the increase.[3] Thus, for example, Greaves, at a meeting of the Manchester Statistical Society in 1863 referred to 'the stories floating in society, of married ladies whenever they find themselves pregnant, habitually beginning to take exercise, on foot or on horseback, to an extent unusual at other times, and thus making themselves abort'.[4] Similarly, Sir James Simpson in 1867 repeated the allegation that 'on the birth of a second or third child, the neighbours will say, "So-and-so has another baby; you'll see it won't live", and that this becomes a sort of joke, in which its mother will join, public opinion expressing no condemnation of her cruelty.'[5]

The editor of the *British Medical Journal* seems to have been especially concerned with this aspect of the problem in his investigations into the practice of baby-farming.

In answer to an advertisement offering a premium for adoption of a child, we received within a week no fewer than three hundred and thirty-three letters, while several personal applications were made during the same period.[6] . . . As the matter now stands, there is not the slightest difficulty in disposing of any number of children, so that they may give no further trouble, and never be heard of, at £10 a head . . . Demand and supply seem to be very equally balanced: and at this time there is certainly a very brisk business.

Hart admitted that many of the children advertised for were genuinely adopted and well looked after, but nevertheless devoted much of his energies for the next ten years to conducting a campaign against baby-farms as centres of infanticide.

Another of his campaigns was directed against 'those hideous excrescences of civilization', professional abortionists.[7] He

3. Banks, *op. cit.*, pp. 149–50. Banks and Glass, *op. cit.*, in Glass ed., *Introduction to Malthus*, pp. 106–11.

4. G. Greaves, *op. cit.*, 1862–3, p. 14.

5. From an abstract of an address by him reported in the *British Medical Journal*, 5 October, 1867, p. 283.

6. The *British Medical Journal*, 28 March, 1868, p. 301. E. A. Hart was the editor from 1866 until his death in 1897. Throughout this period he regularly referred to the subject of baby-farming, and published a pamphlet on it in 1875, see the *British Medical Journal*, 16 January, 1875, p. 84.

7. The *British Medical Journal*, 26 January, 1861, report of a woman found guilty of the wilful murder of a mother of nine children who applied to her for an abortion, p. 97. A similar case involving a married woman, mother of several children was reported in the *B.M.J.* on 23 June, 1866, p. 669.

investigated a place advertising 'temporary retirement' for ladies and found that abortions could be procured there for 50 guineas, plus 20 more for the services of the woman who ran the house. This establishment had been in the business for twenty-seven years and was never short of patients, some of whom 'come back six or seven times'.[8] We are not told how many of these were married women and how many were prostitutes, but the *Saturday Review* at any rate believed that 'many mothers of the lower-middle class in London avail themselves of French precedents to avoid the cares and expenses of maternity', and argued that 'there are other considerations which influence the minds of those likely to become mothers besides the consciousness of illicit love and the fear of its detection'.[9]

There can be little doubt, moreover, that the practice of contraception was spreading during this period. Although most writers in this subject were guarded in their language we can discern, behind the taboo of silence, hints that the birth-control propaganda was not unheeded. Montague Cookson, for example, in an article in the *Fortnightly Review* in 1872 protesting at the 'unnecessary multiplication of children' mentioned 'not a few' who were familiar with the 'moral lesson' to be drawn from his argument, and 'whose daily practice it has long since served to shape'.[10] The evidence to be drawn from such hints as this is, however, strongly reinforced by the actual decline in family size amongst sections of the middle classes, which may be dated, in its beginnings as early as the late 1860's, and was certainly under way by the end of the 1870's.[11] It is clear from the extent of this decline that although open discussion on the subject was discouraged public opinion within the middle classes was in the process of change.

It is against this background that it is necessary to interpret

8. The *British Medical Journal*, 8 February, 1868, pp. 126–7. See also Hart's evidence before the Select Committee on the Protection of Infant Life, reported in the *B.M.J.*, 27 May, 1871, p. 563.
9. 'Seduction and Infanticide', the *Saturday Review*, 20 October, 1866, p. 481.
10. M. Cookson, 'The Morality of Married Life', the *Fortnightly Review*, October, 1872. Cookson himself was in favour of the safe period. See *The Queen v. Charles Bradlaugh, etc.*, p. 162.
11. Papers of the Royal Commission on Population, Vol. 6. D. V. Glass and E. Grebenik, *The Trend and Pattern of Fertility in Great Britain*, 1954, Part I, Appendix 1 to Chapter 6, Table II, p. 131.

the Bradlaugh-Besant trial of 1877. Fifteen years previously
Bradlaugh had written that his support of Malthusian principles
had made him 'the target for every kind of calumny' and affir-
med that he had had more severe and unkind opposition offered
to his opinions of Malthus than to his 'most extreme hetero-
doxy in theology'.[12] For all that, he continued to write on the
subject,[13] and was moved to provide the authorities with a test
case when, in 1877, his publisher, Watts, pleaded guilty to
publishing a 40-year-old pamphlet on birth-control written by
the American, Charles Knowlton.[14] Bradlaugh's motives seem
to have been as much concerned with the freedom of the press
as with the cause of birth-control as such, and there is evidence
that he and Mrs. Besant were aware of the great risk they were
taking. As she wrote later:[15]

It was not the danger of failure, with the prison as penalty, that
gave us pause. It was the horrible misconceptions that we saw might
arise; the odious imputations on honour and purity that would
follow. Could we, the teachers of a lofty morality, venture to face a
prosecution for publishing what would be technically described as an
obscene book, and risk the ruin of our future, dependent as that was
on our fair fame? To Mr. Bradlaugh it meant, as he felt, the almost
certain destruction of his Parliamentary position, the forging by his
own hands of a weapon that in the hands of his foes would be well-
nigh fatal. To me it meant the loss of the pure reputation I prized,
the good name I had guarded—scandal the most horrible a woman
could face.[16]

In Bradlaugh's case these fears were not altogether justified
by the event. In spite of the efforts of his opponents to exploit his
neo-Malthusian view he was returned as a Liberal member of

12. The *National Reformer*, 15 August, 1862, quoted in *Champion of Liberty:
Charles Bradlaugh* (Centenary Volume), Watts, London, 1933, p. 298.
13. Banks and Glass, *op. cit.*, p. 109. Himes, *Medical History*, p. 236 *et seq.*
14. *Fruits of Philosophy; or, the private companion of young married couples*,
1st American edition, New York, 1832.
15. H. B. Bonner, *Charles Bradlaugh: A Record of His Life and Work*, 7th
edition, Unwin, London, 1908, Vol. 2, p. 17. See also C. Bradlaugh and
A. Besant, Preface to *The Queen* v. *Charles Bradlaugh and Annie Besant* (*Specially
Reported*), London, n.d. (1878?).
16. A. Besant, *An Autobiography*, second edition, Unwin, London, 1908,
p. 207. It is very possible that Bradlaugh had in mind the defeat of Lord
Amberley in the South Devon election in 1868, because of his neo-Malthusian views, see Banks, *op. cit.*, pp. 146–9.

Parliament for Northampton in the general election of 1880,
although only after twelve years of unsuccessful campaigning.
Once elected, however, he was faced with six years of bitter
struggle with Parliament itself on the issue of the oath of alle-
giance before he could claim his seat. In this instance opposition
rested mainly on his atheism,[17] but his views on birth-control were also introduced into the controversy and may well
have further embittered the fight.[18] Outside Parliament, too,
he had to face considerable abuse, often of a most vicious kind.
He was alleged, for example, to be connected 'with the filthy
literature of the London streets', and to have been convicted in
a criminal court of disseminating 'printed poison'.[19] Thus if his
career was not, as he had feared, irretrievably wrecked, the prosecution in 1877 undoubtedly added to the difficulties he had
already faced as a convinced atheist.

For Mrs. Besant the consequences were even more serious.
She, too, had to face public abuse, and insinuations of the gros-
sest kinds of immorality, but even worse was the successful
attempt to deprive her of the custody of her young daughter.
She and her husband had separated in 1873, and an agreement had been arrived at which gave custody of the son to the
father, but the daughter, then only three years old, was allowed
to remain with the mother. The double charge of atheism and
Malthusianism was, however, sufficient grounds for a court to
decide that Mrs. Besant was unfit for the custody of a daughter.
Said Lord Justice James:

> It is impossible for us not to feel that the conduct of the appellant
> in writing and publishing such works is so repugnant, so abhorrent,
> to the feelings of the great majority of decent Englishmen and
> Englishwomen, and would be regarded by them with such disgust,
> not as matters of opinion, but as violations of morality, decency, and
> womanly propriety, that the future of a girl brought up in associa-
> tion with such propaganda would be incalculably prejudiced . . .
> If the ward were allowed to remain with the mother it is possible,

17. W. L. Arnstein, 'The Bradlaugh Case: a Reappraisal' in the *Journal
of the History of Ideas*, Vol. 18 (2) April 1957, pp. 261–6.
    18. *Ibid.*, p. 260, and J. M. Robertson, 'The Parliamentary Struggle',
Ch. 3 of Part II, Vol. 2. H. B. Bonner, *op. cit.*, see also p. 387.
    19. *Essays for the People: Two Prize Essays on Liberalism in England and its
Demoralizing Effects on Our National Religion and Liberties, given by W. H.
Peters, Esq.*, 1881, First Prize, W. T. Haines, pp. 18 and 25.

and perhaps not improbable, that she would grow up to be the writer and publisher of such works.[20]

It is difficult, in the changed opinion of today, to comprehend the horror with which the open advocacy of artificial checks to parenthood was received. The grounds for prosecution were that Charles Bradlaugh and Annie Besant had issued a 'certain indecent, lewd, filthy, bawdy and obscene book', and there is no doubt that many, at the time, conceived of the work in precisely these terms.[21] 'The book is, in fact', alleged the *Western Daily Mercury*, 'one of those queer freaks that sprout spontaneously from the imagination of people of the free-love class'. It would lead, it was feared, to results similar to those in America which were 'sapping the virtue of the household, weakening the popular respect for the marriage laws and the sacred character of wedlock'.[22]

Other newspapers were equally outspoken in their comments on what the *Saturday Review* called 'the nasty case'. The *Daily Telegraph* could find no difference between the publishers of 'this vile work' and those who offered poisoned food for sale in the markets or threw deadly drugs into wells and drinking fountains. It was, in the opinion of the *Englishman*, 'the most wicked work that was ever written', while according to the *Evening Standard* 'no poison, moral or material, was ever offered to mankind so evil as this philosophy'.[23] Such comments, while extreme in tone, were, nevertheless, widespread, and by no means over-state the reaction of the more conservative section of the press. Even where the language was more moderate, as in the case of *The Times* the rejection of the views propagated by the *Fruits of Philosophy* was no less complete.[24]

It would, however, be a mistake to conclude that the reaction

20. 'The Besant Case', the *Saturday Review*, 12 April, 1879. The *Saturday Review* itself thought that 'even Mrs. Besant would probably admit that an infant daughter might properly be taken away from her mother, supposing that this mother advocated prostitution or infanticide as useful and praiseworthy practices. In the opinion of the greaty majority of Englishmen and Englishwomen there is no appreciable difference between this and the kind of advocacy to which Mrs. Besant has devoted herself.'

21. The Indictment is given in Glass, *Population Policies, op. cit.* Note X, p. 424.

22. 'Our London Letter', the *Western Daily Mercury*, 23 June, 1877.

23. For references see J. A. Banks and Olive Banks, 'The Bradlaugh-Besant Trial and the English Newspapers', *passim, Population Studies*, Vol. 8, No. 1, July, 1954.

24. Quoted in Banks, *Prosperity and Parenthood*, p. 152.

to the views of Bradlaugh and Besant was one of universal condemnation. Behind the stern strictures of the newspaper editors there is evidence of a genuine interest in birth-control propaganda and a readiness to listen to arguments in its favour. The sale of *Fruits of Philosophy* increased enormously even before the trial began and continued at a high level afterwards. People flocked to attend the hearings and subscribed over £1,000 to the public appeal for the defence.[25] Charles Bradlaugh and Annie Besant addressed meetings during and after the trial and were received enthusiastically in packed halls.[26] There was, too, the 'passionate gratitude' expressed by 'letters from thousands of poor married women—many from the wives of country clergymen and curates—thanking and blessing me for showing them how to escape from the veritable hell in which they lived.'[27] The resuscitated Malthusian League enrolled 220 members in its first week and began a campaign to propagate family limitation through lectures, pamphlets and house-to-house canvassing which resulted in the issue of some 3 million pamphlets and leaflets during the next forty years.[28]

There can be no doubt that the success of this movement resulted from the fact that, as compared with the period before 1870, a sufficiently large section of the public was eager for information on the subject. This does not mean that the public taboo was raised from discussions of contraception. Mrs. Besant has herself drawn attention to what the trial cost her in terms of loss of friends and social ostracism, as well as the loss of her daughter.[29] Those who bought birth-control literature or carried out contraceptive techniques did so discreetly.[30]

25. A. Besant, *Autobiography*, p. 231.

26. Banks, *op. cit.*, pp. 153–4, Banks and Banks, p. 32. Ritchie, *Days and Nights in London*, 1880, commented that Bradlaugh's meetings at the Hall of Science were always filled although the seats cost from 3d. to 1s., while the churches were empty.

27. Besant, *op. cit.*, pp. 223–4.

28. Glass, *op. cit.*, pp. 35–43.

29. *Lucifer*, July, 1891, p. 397, quoted in Glass, *op. cit.*, p. 56.

30. J. M. Robertson, *Over-Population*, 1890, p. 20, refers to information being given privately, by letter. Violet Markham, in her autobiography, refers to her mother's sympathy with Charles Bradlaugh and Annie Besant 'at a time when no abuse was bad enough for them. After her death I found a packet of books on free thought and one on birth-control, locked up in a drawer seldom opened.' V. R. Markham, *Return Passage*, Oxford University Press, 1953, p. 22. Her mother died in 1922, see p. 99.

Nevertheless, the falling birth-rate for the upper-middle classes during and after the 1870's is sufficient evidence that in this section of the community family limitation was fully accepted as part of married life.[31]

The 1870's were, therefore, significant both for the gradual, if underground, spread of the practice of family limitation and for the widespread discussion of the idea of birth-control, which was precipitated by the publicity of the Bradlaugh-Besant trial. Nevertheless, the feminist movement, in all its aspects, stood aloof from the controversy. Amongst all the causes with which it was concerned during these years there is no sign of any interest in birth-control, either in its wider implications for population growth, or in its possible effect on the employment of women. The Bradlaugh-Besant trial was totally ignored by the two leading feminist journals, the *Victoria Magazine* and the *Englishwoman's Review*, and the whole subject, whether by accident or design, was scarcely ever mentioned, however discreetly, in their pages. The sole exception is an extract which appeared in the *Victoria Magazine* for November, 1872, reprinted from the *Examiner*, which suggested:

that people are beginning to discover that they are Malthusians without having been aware of it . . . it is more than probable that the pressure of over-population, the one and only cause of all misery and unhappiness, may begin before long to sensibly decrease.[32]

Silence does not, of course, in itself necessarily imply dissent, but there are some indications that the leaders of the movement were on the whole hostile. This, for example, was certainly the position of Millicent Garrett Fawcett and her husband Henry Fawcett. When Bradlaugh wished them to testify formally at the hearing that the general doctrine of family limitation was to be found in works like Fawcett's own *Manual of Political Economy* as part of the general treatment of economic questions, Fawcett protested in the strongest terms, even threatening to send his wife out of the country rather than that she should appear

---

31. Cf. W. T. Stead, 'I have from the birth of Willie (1875?) practised simple syringing with water. Of late always withdrawal. We never used anything but this. . . We had never decided definitely to stop breeding', Diary, 20 January, 1899, quoted in J. W. R. Scott, *The Life and Death of a Newspaper*, 1952, ch. 19.

32. 'The Selfishness of Husbands', p. 91.

as a witness in the case.[33] A letter written by Mrs. Fawcett to Bradlaugh stated their position quite unequivocally. She referred to the 'very strong opinions which Mr. Fawcett entertains as to the objectionable character of the work you have published' an opinion 'so far as my knowledge of the book enables me to speak' with which she agreed entirely; and claimed that 'if we were called as witnesses we should effectually damage your case'.[34]

Hostile, too, to the subject of birth-control was the first woman doctor, Elizabeth Blackwell. She wrote:

The very grave national danger of teaching men to repudiate fatherhood, and welcoming women to despise motherhood and shrink from the trouble involved in the bearing and nurturing of children, demands the most serious consideration.[35]

Although a pioneer in the advocacy of sex education[36] she thought that:

artifices to indulge a husband's sensuality while counteracting Nature is on the one hand most uncertain of success, on the other hand is eminently noxious to the *woman*.[37]

There were, it is true, some who took a different view. Mrs. Besant herself wrote a small book on the case for contraception[38] and published a pamphlet on the political rights of women.[39] Mrs. Fenwick Miller, a member of the London School Board, wrote a letter to the newspapers on behalf of Charles Bradlaugh

33. H. B. Bonner, *op. cit.*, Vol. 2, p. 23.

34. June, 1877, quoted in R. Strachey, *Millicent Garrett Fawcett*, 1913, pp. 88–9.

35. Footnote to the pamphlet by F. W. Newman, *The Corruption Now Called Neo-Malthusianism*, written by request for the Moral Reform Union, with notes by Dr. E. Blackwell, 1889.

36. *The Moral Education of the Young, Considered under Medical and Social Aspects*, 1876, see E. Blackwell, *Pioneer Work for Women*, 1895, Everyman Edition, 1914, pp. 202–3. R. Baker, *The First Woman Doctor: the story of Elizabeth Blackwell*, 1946, p. 177.

37. F. W. Newman, *op. cit.*, italics in the original. These are Newman's own words, but the reference is to Dr. Elizabeth Blackwell 'amongst other physicians'. She had lectured on 'Neo-Malthusianism' in 1888, see her *Medical Sociology*, 1902.

38. *The Law of population: its consequences, and its bearing upon human conduct and morals*, 1878.

39. *The Political Status of Women*, 1875.

and Annie Besant at the time of the trial;[40] and Alice Vickery, one of the earliest of women doctors, although not active generally in the feminist movement was pre-eminent, with her husband Charles Drysdale, in the activities of the Malthusian League. Moreover, in Lord and Lady Amberley we find active support of feminine principles combined with at least some degree of sympathy for neo-Malthusianism.[41] But these are names which are not prominent in the standard histories of the women's movement. The people at the centre who provided the driving energy for the struggle to open up new fields for women's employment, to extend the opportunities for their education into public schools and universities, to obtain the vote—these people had no support to offer to the question of family limitation.

Of course it might be held that this was partly caution on their part. We have already seen that the subject was not one likely to win its advocates other than a most unpleasant notoriety in the 'respectable' quarter of society, and the near success of the political movement in the 1870's might well have led the feminists to avoid a dangerous subject for fear of jeopardizing the support they had already gained.[42] Certainly, it is the case that some of the feminist leaders were concerned about the effect on the struggle for enfranchisement likely to be brought about by women giving support to the campaign initiated by Mrs. Josephine Butler in the early 1870's. This was aimed at the repeal of the Contagious Diseases Acts of 1864–9 which required, in seventeen garrison towns, the registration and police supervision of women suspected of being prostitutes, their periodical medical examination for the detection of venereal disease, and their compulsory detention in special hospitals if diseased. There had been opposition to this measure from the start, but when in 1869 the suggestion was made that the system should be extended further, an appeal was made to Mrs.

40. See the attack on her in 'Women in Council', the *Saturday Review*, 26 April, 1879. She was still Miss Florence Miller at the time of the Bradlaugh-Besant trial.

41. B. and P. Russell, *The Amberley Papers*, Woolf, London, Vol. 1, p. 36, Vol. 2, pp. 170–1, 331–54.

42. A woman's suffrage bill was brought into Parliament and debated every year in the 1870's except 1874, see R. Fulford, *Votes for Women, the Story of a Struggle*, Faber & Faber, London, 1957, p. 82.

Butler who had long been interested in rescue work amongst prostitutes and who was known to be opposed to the Acts.[43] The campaign that followed under her general leadership and inspiration lasted for seventeen years before it was brought to a successful conclusion by the repeal of the Acts.[44]

The nature of the problem and of the arguments that had to be used to support their case created difficulties for women who entered into this controversy. The subject of prostitution was not one to allow of easy discussion, especially in mixed company, and those women who found the temerity to take part in the struggle were met with horrified disgust. The campaign, it was argued in the House of Commons, 'assumed such a form, that it was a disgrace to the country, as it flooded gentlemen's breakfast tables with abominable literature, not addressed to themselves only, but also to their wives and daughters'.[45] The supporters of the repeal were also taken to task for the 'free and unembarrassed kind of talk' that went on between men and women and even amongst unmarried girls who:

give their opinion in public on questions of which it is only charitable to suppose they understand neither the significance nor the propriety . . . The instinct of mankind which has always held the purity of the maiden, and her comparative ignorance of the grosser things of life, as a sacred and lovely thing, is more to be trusted than the defiant daring of a small sect who would have nothing sacred, nothing veiled, nothing hidden.[46]

It is not surprising, therefore, to find the leaders of the women's movement viewing the development of the campaign with some alarm. The teachers, and those working for the extension of educational opportunities to women, were in a particularly difficult position, and practically all those in this field felt it impossible to support the campaign personally.[47] A similar

43. A. S. G. Butler, *Portrait of Josephine Butler*, Faber & Faber, London, 1954, pp. 44–5.
44. For details of the campaign see *ibid.*, Ch. 4 *et seq.*; Strachey, *op. cit.*, Ch. 10. M. G. Fawcett and E. M. Turner, *Josephine Butler: her Work and Principles*, London, 1927. J. L. and Barbara Hammond, *James Stansfield*, London, 1932, and J. E. Butler, *Personal Reminiscences of a Great Crusade*, 1896.
45. Speech of Osborne Morgan against the Women's Disabilities Removal Bill, 1 May, 1872, *Hansard*, Vol. 211, p. 56.
46. 'Dirt-Pies', the *Saturday Review*, 26 February, 1870.
47. Strachey, *op. cit.*, pp. 197–8.

difficulty faced those in the suffrage field, particularly when it became apparent that the agitation for the repeal of the Acts was in danger of losing the suffrage movement support. One member of Parliament indeed, publicly attributed his loss of faith in the enfranchisement of women directly to this campaign which, so he believed, was on a subject which women ought never to touch upon in public. 'He looked upon their conduct respecting that movement as a foretaste of what the country might expect if women were engaged largely in politics.'[48]

Concern to keep the political movement apart from the repeal movement resulted, in fact, in a split in the ranks of the suffragists, and for six years there were two bodies organizing the campaign for the vote. By 1877, however, the strength had gone out of the opposition to Mrs. Butler's crusade, and the enfranchisement movement became unified once more. It is doubtful, however, whether the general public ever became aware of this split, and women worked equally enthusiastically for both causes. Indeed, apart from the majority of women doctors, who followed the medical profession generally in its support for the Acts, there can be little doubt that the great bulk of the feminists were behind the Repeal, even if they were not prepared openly to say so for political reasons.[49] It was recognized, as the *Englishman's Review* pointed out twenty years later, as part of the general cause.

Side by side with the sustained effort to raise up a safe causeway, so to say, along which women might tread firm and secure towards the attainment of solid knowledge and honourable work, there has run throughout the whole time another effort, parallel in its course, but different in character. If the one has striven to build a causeway, the other has striven to drain a slough—the Slough of Despond of immorality and vice. The two lines of effort are distinct, but they are in harmony: one is constructive of good, the other is destructive of evil. Both are needed; the workers in the one often cross over to the other, although the work runs separate. Thus it comes to pass that this Review, devoted as it is to the constructive side, is naturally comparatively silent, though far from indifferent to that work which Mrs. Butler so aptly sums up as the Great Crusade.[50]

48. Speech of Mr. Hanbury in the House of Commons, opposing the Women's Disabilities Removal Bill, 6 June, 1877, *Hansard*, Vol. 234, p. 1364.
49. Strachey, *op. cit.*, pp. 198 and 266–71.
50. Review of Mrs. Butler's *Personal Reminiscences of a Great Crusade*, 15 January, 1897.

Silent, in fact, the *Review* never was, for it ignored neither the
campaign for the repeal of the Contagious Diseases Acts, nor
the allied crusade for the protection of young girls from the
dangers of seduction which followed it. In 1885 W. T. Stead,
in his now famous *Maiden Tribute to Modern Babylon* had 'electri-
fied the moral conscience of the country'.[51] In these sensational
articles, he revealed the extent of the purchase of young girls
and the ease with which it would be accomplished, by himself
buying nine children within ten days for less than £30. He
described the business of procuring, which was quite openly
practised, and the imprisonment in brothels which the law
condoned. His disclosures aroused a storm of protest, not so
much for what he described, as for the fact that he had openly
discussed it; but the facts themselves could not be ignored, and
the law was changed.[52]

It is clear, therefore, that where it was believed to be necessary, 'unsavoury' subjects did, however unwillingly, become a
part of the feminist cause, and those women who could not
themselves take an active part in the controversy gave their
silent approval. Against this background the almost total boy-
cott concerning birth-control leads strongly to the conclusion
that the feminists as a whole were, if not entirely hostile,
relatively indifferent to the topic. Certainly they did not see it
as a problem which needed their crusading zeal and Annie
Besant, in spite of her feminist views, has never become one of
the heroines of the movement.[53]

The years between 1870 and 1900, on the other hand, witnessed a gradual change in the attitude towards the discussion
of topics which might be considered 'unsavoury'. Thus middle-
class newspapers and ladies' journals began to carry details
of divorce cases in the 1880's and 1890's, whereas previously
they had left them to the more 'popular' Sunday newspapers

51. The *Englishwoman's Review*, 15 August, 1885. See also 'Protection of
Young Girls', a report on the demonstrations in Hyde Park, the *Englishwoman's
Review*, 15 September, 1885.
52. See the *Pall Mall Gazette*, 6 and 12 July, 1885. E. W. Stead, *My
Father: Personal and Spiritual Reminiscences* (n.d.), J. W. R. Scott, *op. cit.*,
Ch. 13.
53. It is perhaps significant, that the *Englishwoman's Review* passed over in
silence the Besant case of 1879 when Mrs. Besant lost the custody of her
daughter, although it readily reported other, similar cases.

who treated them as 'scandalous and salacious copy'.[54] By the end of the century it appears to have become possible to write more freely about sexual problems, and the question of family limitation could no longer be ignored, now that the decline of the birth-rate amongst the middle classes was a recognized fact. This is not to say that there was not considerable opposition to the principle of 'artificial checks to population' or contraceptive techniques.

The medical profession as a whole has set its face against such practices, which are unnatural and degrading in their mental effect, and ofttimes injurious to both husband and wife in their physical results. A small number of medical men have held and taught other views, but the evil has been chiefly caused by cheap pamphlets on the subject, and by advertisements in weekly and other newspapers (often so-called religious newspapers) which under a very thin disguise offer facilities for procuring abortion or preventing conception.[55]

The medical profession was not the only body to protest. Within the Church there was also great anxiety. The subject was discussed at the Manchester Church Congress of 1888 when one speaker referred to 'the awful heresy which is prevailing throughout the country as to restraining the growth of population by artificial means'.[56] This 'heresy' was the subject of a tract published by the Moral Reform Union in 1889. Entitled *The Corruption Called Neo-Malthusianism* it argued that 'a new school falsely calling itself Malthusianism, under pretence of benevolence pollutes marriage itself by a foul doctrine'. It demanded 'that those who commend practices which are certainly foul, shall give proof that they are not also as futile and dangerous as honourable members of the Profession assert them to be in their Medical denunciations of them', and concluded 'may we not vehemently implore all women not infatuated and all men not drunk with base appetite to re-

54. G. Rowntree and N. H. Carrier, 'The Resort to Divorce in England and Wales, 1858–1957', *Population Studies*, Vol. 11, No. 3, March, 1958, p. 198. This study includes an examination of a selection of Sunday newspapers, women's weeklies and general interest magazines published in the census years, 1871, 1891, 1911, 1931 and 1951.

55. 'The French and English Birth-Rate', the *British Medical Journal*, 29 June, 1901.

56. Quoted in R. Ussher, *Neo-Malthusianism: an Enquiry into that System with regard to its Economy and Morality*, 1897, p. 11.

nounce the silly idea that any medical cleverness can outwit the broad ordinance of God'.[57]

The view that contraceptive measures were physically harmful as well as morally wrong was the view of the Lambeth Conference of Bishops in 1908. A resolution condemned such means of birth-control in the following outspoken terms.

The Conference regards with alarm the growing practice of the artificial restriction of the family, and earnestly calls upon all Christian peoples to discountenance the use of all artificial means of restriction as demoralizing to character and hostile to national welfare.

The Conference affirms that deliberate tampering with nascent life is repugnant to Christian morality.

The Conference expresses most cordial appreciation of the services rendered by those medical men who have borne courageous testimony against the injurious practices spoken of, and appeals with confidence to them and to their medical colleagues to co-operate in creating and maintaining a wholesome public opinion on behalf of the reverent use of the married state.[58]

But although the Church, in company with much of the medical profession were strongly opposed to birth-control techniques, by the 1890's they had come to accept the need to prevent the evils in marriage arising out of a 'too rapid multiplication of the family', as the *Christian World* put it.

There was a time when any idea of voluntary limitation was regarded by pious people as interfering with Providence. We are beyond that now, and have become capable of recognizing that Providence works through the common sense of individual brains. We limit population just as much by deferring marriage from prudential motives as by any action that may be taken after it . . . Apart from certain methods of limitation, the morality of which is gravely questioned by many, there are certain easily understood physio-logical laws of the subject, the failure to know and to observe which is inexcusable on the part either of men or women in these circumstances.[59]

57. F. W. Newman, *op. cit.*
58. Published in *The Declining Birth-Rate, its Causes and Effects, being the Report of and the chief evidence taken by the National Birth-Rate Commission, instituted, with official recognition, by the National Council of Public Morals—for the Promotion of Race Regeneration—Spiritual, Moral and Physical*, second edition, 1917, p. 388.
59. 15 June, 1893, p. 487, quoted in Glass, *op. cit.*, note jj, pp. 429–30.

Much the same point of view was taken by the Bishops in 1914, in a document produced for private circulation amongst the clergy and workers of the Church of England. Recognizing that 'changes have been silently proceeding which touch some of the most sacred and intimate parts of life,' it advocated 'reasonable and conscientious self-restraint' or, where 'necessity urges' the restriction of sexual intercourse 'by consent to certain times at which it is less likely to lead to conception. This is only to use natural conditions; it is approved by good medical authority; it means self-denial and not self-indulgence. And we believe it to be quite legitimate, or at least not to be condemned.'[60]

In this rather different environment it is to be expected that some of the feminists, at least, would have become advocates of family limitation, even if it were not taken up more widely by the movement. From the 1890's onwards a small but growing number of women began explicitly to link feminism with some form of Malthusianism. One of the most outspoken and untiring advocates of this point of view, at this time, was Mrs. Mona Caird, whose views on freer marriage excited much controversy in the late 1880's.[61] Early in 1890 she wrote an article for the *Fortnightly Review* in which she asked the question:

What is the proportion of children whose mothers were perfectly willing and able to bring them into the world, willing, in a strict sense, apart from all considerations of duty, or fear of unsanctioned sentiment? Do we not see that the mother of half a dozen children, who struggles to cultivate her faculties, to be an intelligent human being, nearly always breaks down under the burden, or shows very marked intellectual limitations?[62]

In 1892, this time in the *Nineteenth Century*, she argued that:

the rights of the existing race are at least as great as those of the coming one. There is something pathetically absurd in the sacrifice to their children of generation after generation of grown people . . .

60. 'The Misuse of Marriage', Memorandum of January, 1914, reproduced in *The Declining Birth-Rate*, pp. 382–8.
61. See her articles, 'Marriage' in the *Westminster Review*, August, 1888 and 'Ideal Marriage', *ibid.*, November, 1888 and the letters to the *Daily Telegraph* in those months.
62. M. Caird, 'The Morality of Marriage', the *Fortnightly Review*, March, 1890, reprinted in M. Caird, *The Morality of Marriage*, 1897.

If the new movement had no other effect than to rouse women to rebellion against the madness of large families, it would confer a priceless benefit on humanity. Let any reasonable woman expend the force that under the old order would have been given to the production of say, the third, fourth, or fifth child, upon work of another kind, and let her also take the rest and enjoyment, whatever her work, that every human being needs.[63]

Mona Caird's argument that women were not free even to refuse to bear children and that if they were, they would bear fewer, seems 'to have shocked some people very much', but she was not alone in her views.[64] Even the *Saturday Review*, in a series of articles in 1895 by a 'Woman of the Day' argued the same case.

The only woman at the present time who is willing to be regarded as a mere breeding machine is she who lacks the wit to adopt any other role, and now she is the exception rather than the rule. That the zenith of her youth should be spent in the meaningless production of children born into a country already over-populated seems to the woman of to-day a sorry waste of vitality ... For the first time since her creation woman has begun to doubt the morality of producing children under unfavourable conditions, children who lack the physical and mental stamina to wrest success from an adverse destiny, or the fortune to buy it on easy terms. Her experience of life and her clearness of judgement teach her that, if she has neither health nor wealth to give her offspring, morality requires her to go childless all her days.[65]

The views of this new kind of women who,

'Conformed to claims of intellect and need
The tempered numbers of their highborn breed'[66]

found their way regularly into verse and fiction during this

63. M. Caird, 'The Defence of the So-called "Wild Women"', the *Nineteenth Century*, May, 1892, reprinted in *The Morality of Marriage*, 1897. An extract from this article has been reproduced in M. Goodwin's anthology of extracts from the first fifty volumes of the review, entitled *Nineteenth-Century Opinion*, Penguin Books, 1951, pp. 91–3.
64. C. Black, 'On Marriage: A Criticism', the *Fortnightly Review*, April, 1890.
65. 'The Maternal Instinct', the *Saturday Review*, 8 June, 1895. See also F. Swiney, *The Awakening of Women*, 1908, pp. 117–9 and p. 211.
66. Ellis Ethelmer, *Woman Free*, published by the Women's Emancipation Union, 1893, stanza 46, p. 23, and notes, pp. 173–8. Ellis Ethelmer, the pseudonym of the secretary of the W.E.U., Mrs. Wolstenholme Elmy–or perhaps of her and her husband, Ben Elmy jointly, also published *The Human Flower*, 1894, a pamphlet on sex education which favoured the safe period, p. 43.

period. Thus, Lady Florence Dixie's heroine, having disguised herself as a man and obtained a seat in the House of Commons, made a speech in favour of the emancipation of women, during the course of which she said:

There is a problem creeping gradually forward upon us, a problem that will have to be solved in time, and that is the steady increase in population . . . I believe that with the emancipation of women we shall solve this problem now. Fewer children will be born, and those that are born will be of a higher and better physique than the present order of men. [67]

The point of view expressed by these and other writers rested in part on biological and eugenic theories as to the health of mother and child, [68] and in part on a new view of the married woman's rights to independent self-development. [69] If Nature intended women to be 'before all things good wives and mothers', [70] as the anti-feminists so frequently asserted, [71] she also intended, retorted the *Englishwoman's Review*, that men should be good husbands.

The woman has as much right to live her individual life before God as the man . . . no man is a good husband who does not respect the individuality of his wife, body, soul, and spirit, as much as his own. [72]

There were, of course, differences of opinion as to the means to be employed to limit the size of families; yet whether they called for 'the exercise of moral self-control on the part of their

67. F. Dixie, *Gloriana, or the Revolution of 1900*, 1890, p. 137. For other examples, see Ussher, *op. cit.*, pp. 66–7, 'The sex novel of the present day, and the revolt against maternity, show what is passing in the minds of many women at the present time. Marriage is to be free love and with no child-life', and examples quoted. See also, E. R. Chapman, *Marriage Questions in Modern Fiction, and other essays*, 1897, and W. W. Smyth, *A Baneful Popular Delusion on the Subject of Motherhood*, 1895.

68. W. L. Blease, *The Emancipation of English Women*, 1910, pp. 208–9.

69. See the symposium, 'Does Marriage Hinder a Woman's Self Development?' in the *Lady's Realm*, March, 1899, and A. Colquhoun, *The Vocation of Woman*, 1913, pp. 3–5.

70. G. Allen, 'Plain Words on the Woman Question', the *Fortnightly Review*, October, 1889.

71. E. L. Linton, 'The Wild Women as Politicians', the *Nineteenth Century*, July, 1891. J. M. Allan, *Woman Suffrage Wrong in Principle and Practice, An Essay*, 1890, p. 131.

72. The *Englishwoman's Review*, 15 November, 1889.

husbands',[73] or, much more rarely, for positive knowledge of 'the power to control parenthood',[74] there were by the 1890's, a number of feminists who publicly argued that 'woman free' would refuse to become the mother of a large family. They were, therefore, explicitly relating the emancipation of women and family limitation as cause and effect, but it would be unwise to infer from this that a true causal relationship existed. Rather was the feminist movement reflecting the tendencies of the time, of which the drive towards family limitation was already well-established before it ever became a part of feminist and near-feminist propaganda.

The same is true of the phenomenon of the period known as the 'New Woman'. She was not a creation of the emancipation movement, although she enjoyed, like all her contemporaries, the benefits to be derived from its work. On the contrary, along with the 'New Spirit', the 'New Humour', the 'New Realism', the 'New Hedonism', the 'New Drama', the 'New Unionism', and the 'New Party', she was a sign of the peculiar spirit of the 1890's.[75] This 'New Woman', it was claimed, 'smokes after dinner with the men; in railway carriages; in public rooms—when she is allowed'.[76] She claimed herself to have an 'intense longing to frequent music-halls and possess latchkeys', and wanted 'the abolition of chaperons on all possible occasions and to enjoy 'friendship between men and girls'.[77]

But these were relatively minor demands and minor peccadilloes. Other critics hinted at wilder forms of behaviour. Even as early as 1881 Frances Power Cobbe, herself a feminist, had warned her readers against:

that neglect of social *bienséances*, that adoption of looser and more 'Bohemian' manners, and, worst of all, that fatal laxity of judgement regarding grave moral transgressions, which have appeared of late years amongst us as the inevitable extravagance of reaction from earlier strictness (and which) constitute, I conceive, deadly perils

73. Swiney, *op. cit.*, p. 211.
74. C. W. Saleeby, *Woman and Womanhood*, 1912, p. 244.
75. H. Jackson, *The Eighteen Nineties, a Review of Art and Ideas at the Close of the Nineteenth Century*, 1913, Ch. 1, 'Fin de Siècle', Penguin Edition, 1939, p. 20.
76. E. L. Linton, 'The Wild Women as Social Insurgents', the *Nineteenth Century*, October, 1891. Goodwin, *op. cit.*, p. 83.
77. K. Cuffe, 'A Reply from the Daughters', the *Nineteenth Century*, March, 1894. Goodwin, *op. cit.*, pp. 85–8.

to the whole movement for the advancement of women. There are women who call themselves 'emancipated' now, who are leading lives if not absolutely vicious, yet loose, unseemly, trespassing always on the borders of vice; women who treat lightly, and as if of small account, the heinous and abominable sins of unchastity and adultery.[78]

To some extent her fears were justified. Opponents of the feminist movement all too frequently ascribed the free behaviour of the new woman to the spread of feminist doctrine and feminist reform. It was the opinion of a writer in the *Quarterly Review*, for example, that the 'insidious process of gradual assimilation of girls' education to boys' ' would lead not only to 'extreme laxity in divorce', to 'the institution of female clergy and to many other aberrations', but also to tendencies which lead women 'to wear men's clothes, to play men's games, to smoke, and to advocate relaxations of the ties of marriage and maternity.'[79]

It is, indeed, certain that the second half of Victoria's reign saw a change in the morals and manners of middle-class girls and women. They were no longer brought up to consider their lives circumscribed by the narrow confines of the home. The 'change from samplers and school rooms to skating rinks, lawn-tennis tournaments, bicycle grounds and suppers after the play at restaurants'[80] brought the girl of the period into closer contact with young men of her own class. Topics of conversation which once were not considered 'proper' for married women even when in the sole company of other married women were now the subject of novels and plays and were eagerly debated by the young of both sexes.[81]

If this was emancipation, however, it was not emancipation

78. F. P. Cobbe, *The Duties of Women, A Course of Lectures*, 1881, pp. iv and 112.

79. 'Women at Oxford and Cambridge', the *Quarterly Review*, October, 1897. Cf. W. J. K. Little, *Holy Matrimony*, 1901, p. 203, 'There has come in amongst many a looser way of thinking of the dignity of woman and her true place in human society, which must be deplored, as it has led in the same direction of moral laxity'. Grant Allen's novel, *The Woman Who Did*, written in 1893, also found room to attack 'that blatant and decadent sect of "advanced women" who talk as though motherhood were a disgrace and a burden', Ch. 13, p. 145.

80. T. H. S. Escott, *Social Transformations of the Victorian Age*, 1877, pp. 203–4.

81. H. Jackson, *op. cit.*, p.. 126.

as the feminist movement understood it, and some of its most ardent members protested that 'those who hold the views popularly attributed to the New Woman are most dangerous allies'.[82] No doubt there was some truth in the criticism that the New Woman neglected her home and her children but this attack really applied to 'the butterfly women. The private lives of our advanced women will bear the utmost scrutiny. But look at the silly women who lead objectless lives. They think there is no harm in idling away the morning, spending all the after-noon in society calls, returning home to dress, then out again for the whole evening. . . .'[83] There was truth in the claim that women were refusing motherhood but 'this is far truer of the more pleasure-loving woman to whom the Woman's Movement means nothing than it is of those of whom it is composed'.[84] Of course the size of the family was 'diminishing rapidly, but away with the cant! The real motives are to be found in the fact that modern life, with its pleasures and perpetual amuse-ments, does not harmonize with the claims of maternity.'[85]

Proof that the emancipated or advanced woman in the femi-nist sense of the term was not more likely to limit her family than her unemancipated contemporary is neatly provided by two surveys undertaken at this time. The first was made by Mrs. Henry Sidgwick in the late 1880's and consisted of a comparison of the lives of women students of Oxford and Cambridge with those of their sisters.[86] She concluded that the figures did not support the contention that the college-educated women had smaller families.[87] The second was an enquiry carried out by Dr. Agnes Savill and Dr. Major Greenwood, Jnr., in 1914 for the National Birth-Rate Commission on a similar group of college women and their sisters or relatives, with the same results as Mrs. Sidgwick.[88]

82. Mrs. A. H. Bright in an interview with Sarah Tooley published in 'Ladies of Liverpool, 2', the *Woman at Home,* June, 1895.
83. *Ibid.,* Interview of Mrs. E. Stewart-Brown.
84. Z. Fairfield, 'The Christian Ethic and the Individual' in Z. Fairfield, ed., *Some Aspects of the Woman's Movement,* 1915, p. 171.
85. Lady Jeune, 'Rejoinder' to 'The Maternal Instinct', the *Saturday Review,* 8 June, 1895.
86. H. Sidgwick, *Health Statistics of Women Students of Cambridge and Oxford and of their Sisters,* Cambridge University Press, 1890.
87. *The Declining Birth-Rate,* p. 19.
88. *Ibid.,* pp. 19–21, 322–5.

The available evidence, therefore, leads unmistakably to the conclusion that the movement towards family limitation proceeded quite independently of the efforts of the feminists, who in this respect were prepared to follow the fashion of their time, even where they disapproved of some of the reasons for following it. They did not, that is to say, see the burden of child-bearing as a problem until the smaller family was already an established fact amongst the middle classes, and even then there were few in their ranks who publicly supported the neo-Malthusian cause. As we have seen this apparent indifference can hardly be attributed merely to squeamishness on their part, as they were prepared to risk unpopularity by dealing with sexual questions if they saw fit. The bulk of the feminist movement was behind Josephine Butler in her crusade against the Contagious Diseases Acts. Why then was the Bradlaugh-Besant trial and the neo-Malthusian controversy so pointedly ignored? It must be assumed that the silence on the part of the feminists concealed opposition rather than mere indifference. To understand why this was so we must look rather more closely at the nature of their attitude to sexual morality.

CHAPTER 8

The Attitude to Sex

IN their plea for a greater measure of equality between men and women the nineteenth-century feminists did not overlook the area in which inequality was to be found in perhaps its most extreme form—the double standard of morality. The fight against this particular inequality was, at times at least, as central to the movement as its campaigns for higher education for girls or the struggle for the vote. It is of some importance, therefore, to consider briefly the meaning of this double standard and the restrictions it imposed upon the lives of women. In its most obvious form it involved, as is well known, the imposition of a far stricter sexual morality upon middle-class women than upon the men of the same class. Chastity, both before and after marriage, was regarded as desirable for a man, but it was a necessity for any woman who wished to retain even the semblance of respectability. The Matrimonial Causes Act of 1857 clearly recognized this philosophy, making it possible for a husband to petition for divorce on the ground of his wife's adultery alone, but requiring her to prove desertion, cruelty, incest, rape, sodomy or bestiality as well.

During the course of the debate on the Bill the Lord Chancellor defended this attitude towards female chastity on the basis of social expediency.

> A wife might, without any loss of caste, and possibly with reference to the interests of her children, or even of her husband, condone an act of adultery on the part of the husband; but a husband could not condone a similar act on the part of a wife. No one would venture to suggest that a husband could possibly do so, and for this, among other reasons . . . that the adultery of the wife might be the means of palming spurious offspring upon the husband, while the adultery of the husband could have no such effect with regard to the wife.[1]

Less brutal but no less expedient arguments were continually

1. *Hansard*, 1857, Vol. 145, col. 813, quoted in O. R. McGregor, *Divorce in England, op. cit.*, p. 20.

put forward to support the double standard. The *Saturday Review* asserted that in 1869:

> Whether women can understand it or not as long as society exists, incontinence on man's part will be compared with incontinence on woman's part, not as a matter solely of personal right, which here means personal wrong, but as a matter of public policy. On ethical grounds, the sin is the same in the one case as in the other: on social considerations, the adultery of the wife is, and always will be, a more serious matter than the infidelity of the husband.[2]

Moreover, the double standard, in practice, covered a much wider field than the single insistence on female chastity. It was because they believed that the very knowledge of sexual immorality was harmful to their womenfolk that the Victorians banished sexual topics from their drawing-rooms and exerted a stern censorship on those publications which were for mixed reading. The novelist who was too outspoken for his, or her, readers had to expect a storm of indignant letters and shocked protest. This was the fate of Mrs. Gaskell's *Ruth* in 1853,[3] and of George Moore's *Esther Waters* in 1894,[4] to mention only two cases. Even the hint that a wife might commit adultery was considered by some to be going too far. Trollope, it may be remembered, gave an account of a letter received from a clergyman during the serial publication of *Can You Forgive Her* in 1863, complaining on this score.

> It had been one of the innocent joys of his life, said the clergyman, to have my novels read to him by his daughters. But now I was writing a book which caused him to bid them close it! Must I also turn away to vicious sensation such as this? Did I think that a wife contemplating adultery was a character fit for my pages?[5]

With this in mind it is easier to understand why the activities of the feminists were so often seen as a threat to the sanctity of marriage and home. All the successive steps towards emancipation were perceived by their opponents as imperilling woman's special character as the custodian of the 'walled garden' or the 'angel in the house' and all for the same reason, that they

2. 'Woman's Rights in New York', the *Saturday Review*, 6 February, 1869.
3. P. Thomson, *The Victorian Heroine: A Changing Ideal, 1837–1873*, Oxford University Press, 1956, pp. 131–5.
4. H. Jackson, *op. cit.*, p. 41.
5. A. Trollope, *An Autobiography, 1883*, Ch. 10, World Classics Edition, Oxford University Press, p. 157.

would lead to an extension of her knowledge of evil. 'It is no small thing that half the human race should habitually take a purer and more sentimental view of life than those who have to do the dirty work', argued the *Saturday Review*, in the course of a suggestion that to give women the vote was 'to endanger the institution of marriage and the family'.[6]

The fear that women would be corrupted by knowledge was revealed, above all, in the reaction to Josephine Butler and the campaign for the repeal of the Contagious Diseases Acts. 'We learn from their Petitions and their statements that they "thoroughly understand the subject" and know the effect it has alike on the physical and moral health of the community', declared one of the opponents of the campaign in the House of Commons. 'That is one of the effects of the entrance of women in political life. The question is, whether you would wish to see it extended, and, if so, to what extent, for to what it might lead us no one can tell.'[7]

It is, indeed, possible that one of the consequences of the campaign for the repeal of the Contagious Diseases Acts was that it spread amongst the respectable and hitherto ignorant women in the community an awareness of those evils which, in Josephine Butler's own words 'bore with murderous cruelty on other women';[8] but if this were so, it was not the aim the campaigners had in mind. They circulated information merely in order to strengthen their case for repeal, and to put an end to the double standard. Nor was it their intention that a single standard of morality should take the form of women becoming as libertine and profligate as the men. They were not in revolt against the traditional view that the good woman equally with the good wife was 'strictly and conscientiously virtuous, constant, and faithful to her husband, chaste, pure and unblemished, in every thought, word and deed'.[9] On the contrary,

6. 'Women's Votes', the *Saturday Review*, 6 May, 1871. See also the review article on 'The Subjection of Women', the *Saturday Review*, 19 June, 1869.

7. Speech of Sir Henry James on the Women's Disabilities Removal Bill, 7 April, 1875, *Hansard*, Vol. 223, p. 452.

8. George W. and Lucy A. Johnson (eds.), *Josephine Butler: An Autobiographical Memoir*, Arrowsmith, Bristol, 2nd edition, 1911, p. 31.

9. T. Moore, *Marriage Customs and Modes of Courtship*, op. cit., 1820, 'The Character of a Good Wife', p. 360.

their aim was to strengthen this concept of morality by preventing men from undermining it.

It is true that in taking up the cause of the prostitute they were going counter to the norms of feminine behaviour, but their action, in their own eyes, was perfectly consistent with the strictest virtue. They might be ready, and indeed eager, to assist their 'fallen sister', but they were not prepared to condone her sin.

At the same time in spite of their acceptance of the masculine view of feminine purity they did not thereby relinquish their demand for equality. The double standard of sexual morality was attacked vigorously and frequently, but the professed alternative was not greater freedom for women but greater self-control for men. The standard of purity which applied to the respectable middle-class woman could, and should be applied equally to both sexes before marriage and after. This claim was fundamental to the movement for the repeal of the Contagious Diseases Acts, and the agitation which followed it against white-slave traffic. It is also revealed, quite unambiguously, in the following petition which the Moral Reform Union presented to the House of Lords in 1884.

That having before them the fact that women are constantly annoyed and imperilled by the solicitation of profligate men in the streets and elsewhere, your Petitioners humbly pray that your Honourable House will, in justice, make the male offender in this matter of solicitation equally punishable with the female offender, against whom laws now exist; and that in all future legislation the same principle of equality between the sexes shall be observed.[10]

Above all the campaign was an attempt to combat 'the assumption that indulgence is a necessity of man'[11] and put forward instead 'the better and true belief that vice was capable of diminution, and that law and government ought to be on the side of virtue'.[12] Those who opposed the Acts believed that by the acceptance of State regulation of prostitution 'the path of evil is made more easy to our sons, and to the whole of the

---

10. Quoted in the *Englishwoman's Review*, 15 March, 1884.
11. Speech of Mr. Fowler on the Contagious Diseases Act, Repeal Bill, 21 May, 1873, *Hansard*, Vol. 216, p. 233.
12. Sir James Stansfield in the House of Commons, 16 March, 1886, *Hansard*, Vol. 303, p. 984.

youth of England; inasmuch as a moral restraint is withdrawn the moment the State recognizes, and provides convenience for the practice of a vice which it thereby declares to be necessary and venial.[13]

In order to understand the full implication of the feminist position it is necessary to emphasize, at this point, that in their eyes at least, woman was almost always the victim of man's sexual desires. The Contagious Diseases Acts were not only held to be immoral, they were also unfair because 'it is unjust to punish the sex who are the victims of a vice, and leave unpunished the sex who are the main cause, both of the vice and its dreaded consequences'.[14] Even a married woman, if she had any pretentions to virtue, was at the most a passive recipient of her husband's demands which, furthermore, seem to have been seen not as a natural and necessary biological drive, but as an unhappy indication of the 'beast in human nature'.[15] Some, indeed, went so far as to claim that menstruation itself was a pathological and unnatural state, which had been brought about by man's excessive and brutal sexuality.

> Action repeated tends to rhythmic course,
> And thus the mischief due at first to force,
> Brought cumulative sequence to the race,
> Till habit bred hereditary trace;
> On woman falls that heritage of woe,
> And e'en the virgin feels its dastard blow.[16]

In its extreme form this wing of the movement appeared 'to abhor and belittle the whole idea of sex'.[17] Moreover, spinster-

---

13. Josephine E. Butler, *Personal Reminiscences of a Great Crusade*, Horace Marshall, London, New Edition, 1911, p. 10, from the Women's Protest, published in the *Daily News*, 1 January, 1870.

14. *Ibid.*, p. 9.

15. 'A Dark Shadow', the *Englishwoman's Review*, 15 July, 1897.

16. Ellis Ethelmer, *Woman Free*, 1893, stanza 23. Mr. and Mrs. Elmy seem to have believed that the ultimate success of the Women's Rights Movement would put an end to menstruation since doctors would come to regard it as a disease and look for a cure. Stanza 28. Once this 'lingering mark of man's unthinking guilt and shame' was removed, true equality between the sexes would be possible, for woman's mind would be able to develop with 'newer vigour' when her body was 'saved from enervating drain'. Stanzas 32 and 33. See also the notes to these stanzas at the end of the poem.

17. Z. Fairfield, *Some Aspects of the Women's Movement*, op. cit., p. 170.

hood, once a dreaded fate, was now endured not only with
equanimity but from choice, as more and more women dis-
covered the joys of independence.

Whatever may be said by narrow-minded biologists, who apparently cannot regard a woman except as a female animal, we maintain
that facts reveal to us the existence of a certain number of women
who, in their own estimation at least, are happier and better as
spinsters than wives.[18]

Indeed it was even suggested that:

the modern dislike of the celibate has its root in the natural annoy-
nace of an over-sexed and mentally-lax generation at receiving
ocular demonstration of the fact that animal passions can be kept
under control.[19]

Within the militant suffrage movement itself we find the
clearest sign of a 'sex-war' which saw man as the inferior and
the enemy. These views were expressed in perhaps their most
extreme form in what has been called 'one of the strangest
documents in pre-war English History'.[20] This was a pamphlet
by Christabel Pankhurst reprinted from *The Suffragette* in 1913
which stated categorically that 'sexual diseases are the great
cause of physical, mental, and moral degeneracy, and of race
suicide. As they are very widespread (from 75 to 80 per cent of
men being infected by gonorrhoea, and a considerable per-
centage, difficult to ascertain precisely, being infected with
syphilis), the problem is one of appalling magnitude.'[21] The
intention of the pamphlet was to act as 'a warning to women
of the grave dangers of marriage so long as the moral standards
of men continue to be lower than their own'. There should be
'no mating between the spiritually developed woman of this
new day and men who in thought or conduct with regard to
sex matters are their inferiors'.[22] But the objection was not
simply that the great majority of men were physically diseased.
Their whole attitude to sex was at fault. 'The truth is', she

18. 'Normal or Abnormal', the *Englishwoman's Review*, 14 December, 1889.
19. C. Hamilton, *Marriage as a Trade*, new and cheaper edition, 1912,
p. 204.
20. G. Dangerfield, *The Strange Death of Liberal England*, Constable,
London, 1936, p. 190.
21. C. Pankhurst, *The Great Scourge and how to end it*, 1913, p. vi.
22. *Ibid.*, pp. 44 and 98.

asserted, 'that the desires of men are inflamed to an unnatural degree by impure thought and action, by excess in the way of meat and drink, and by physical and mental indolence'. Accordingly, one of the lessons that men have to learn is that their sex powers are given to them as a trust to be used, 'not for the purposes of immorality and debauchery, but to be used reverently and in a union based on love, for the purpose of carrying on the race'.[23] The Vote, it appeared, in Dangerfield's words 'was something between a prophylactic and a call to the higher life'.[24]

There is in all this perhaps a hint of homosexuality,[25] and it would be unwise to think of the feminist movement wholly in terms of sex warfare. Nevertheless, the slogan of 1913—'Votes for Women and Purity for Men'—is not an unexpected outcome of the ideas expressed in the writings of the feminists from the 1870's onwards. There can be no doubt that many of them thought of the future society as one in which 'marriage would be a fellowship of comrades', and that relationships of a 'crudely and purely physical' kind would be replaced by 'psychic and intellectual' love. The New Woman in this sense looked forward to being matched with a New Man.[26]

This, however, was a much later, although logically consistent, development of the attack on the double standard as it had been expressed in the 1860's and 1870's. Its importance in the present context, should not for that reason be underestimated; for quite apart from its intrinsic interest as a feature of feminism as such, it is significant for the light it throws on the fact that the feminists in the crucial years maintained an otherwise surprising reticence on the subject of birth-control. It will be recalled that the defence of the double standard was maintained on the grounds of social expediency, and the existence of the prostitute defended on the grounds of necessity, the result of a conflict between the organization of society and man's sexual appetites. In a dramatic passage Lecky put the case to

23. *Ibid.,* pp. 121 and 123.
24. *Op. cit.,* p. 191.
25. Dangerfield, *op. cit.,* p. 142, 'it was from some secret yearning to recover the wisdom of women that the homosexual movement first manifested itself, in 1912, among the suffragettes'.
26. O. Schreiner, *Woman and Labour,* 1911, pp. 253–8.

which the feminists were opposed in its most insidious form. The prostitute, he said, was:

ultimately the most efficient guardian of virtue. But for her, the un-challenged purity of countless happy homes would be polluted, and not a few who, in the pride of their untempted chastity, think of her with an indignant shudder would have known the agony of remorse and despair.[27]

Moreover, the increase in prostitution, which was attracting so much attention at this time, was seen to be a consequence of the growing practice of postponing marriage.[28] Prudently awaiting the proper time to marry, the young men of the middle classes had recourse, meanwhile, to prostitution.

They will not marry, but they do not lead a life of celibacy; it is notorious that they do not . . . they provide themselves with the physical indulgences of love at what they consider a cheaper rate and as for the sentiment and affection of love, they value those too little to be willing to pay the necessary price. They can afford themselves a mistress, but not a wife.[29]

We have already discussed the motives for postponing marriage. A man did not marry until he could afford to maintain his wife in a 'fitting establishment'.

The man who marries before he is in receipt of an ample income, and who has to face the struggles which await the poor, is considered to lose caste. Virtue is good, but a house in Belgravia is better. Parents would sooner connive at illicit amours in the case of their sons, than see them plunged into the narrow circumstances with their manifold difficulties, and privations, in which they would be involved did they marry on a slender income.[30]

It is not surprising, therefore, to find those most anxious about the

27. W. E. H. Lecky, *History of European Morals*, 10th edition, 1892, Vol. 2, p. 283.

28. See, for example, W. Acton, *Prostitution, considered in its Moral, Social and Sanitary Aspects, in London and other large cities, with proposals for the Mitigation and Prevention of its Attendant Evils*, London, 1857. *SOCIAL versus POLITICAL REFORM: The Sin of Great Cities, or the Great Social Evil: a National Sin, illustrated by a brief enquiry into its extent, causes, effects, and existing remedies*, London, 1859. B. Hemyng, 'Prostitution in London', in H. Mayhew, ed., *London Labour and the London Poor*, London, 1862, Vol. 4.

29. 'The Social Sores of Britain', the *North British Review*, December, 1867, article 8, p. 529.

30. J. E. Forster, *The Divorce Court*, 1888, p. 25, and also J. M. Robertson, *Over-Population*, 1890, p. 16.

spread of prostitution advocating earlier marriage as a remedy.

It has almost become a positive moral duty to incite people to get rid of those faithful cautions, and selfish maxims, which deter young people from wedlock. Matrimony should be a necessary change in the life of a young man, and not, as it now is, a matter of worldly prudence and convenience. Why should young men live on from year to year in immoral bachelorhood, when a little sacrifice of family pride, vanity and fashion, would enable them, with care, to keep a wife and family in comfort, if not in affluence? If people were taught to be content with a sufficiency instead of having their hearts set upon obtaining fortunes, there would be far less of immorality in the world. Purity of life with the mass, without marriage, is an impossibility: and marriage, to be pure, ought not to be deferred till late in life.[31]

Yet simple exhortation was unlikely to be successful at a time when later marriages were becoming increasingly the rule. One writer, consequently, suggested the sanction of a bachelor tax, to be imposed at the age of twenty-one, but this idea does not seem to have been taken up more widely.[32] Nor does it appear likely that even such a positive measure as this would have prevailed. Earlier marriages normally entailed larger families and all that these implied in terms of household expenses, servants, and the cost of living generally. Short of having recourse to contraception or accepting a lower standard of living, the man who made an early marriage was still faced with the alternatives of prostitution or self-restraint.

It was to provide a solution to this dilemma that the neo-Malthusians suggested contraception by mechanical means, or, as it was termed by George Drysdale 'preventive intercourse'.

It is granted that preventive intercourse is unnatural, but the circumstances of our life leave us no alternative. If we were to obey all the natural impulses, and follow our sexual desires like the inferior animals, which live a natural life, we would be forced to prey upon and check the growth of each other, just as they do. We must of

31. *Social versus Political Reform*, p. 13. The same type of argument was still being used forty years later, see R. ff. Blake, *The Greatest Temptation in the World to Man*, London, 1894, pp. 14 and 42.

32. S. A. Sewell, *op. cit.*, pp. 67–9. The *Weekly Dispatch* of 22 January, 1860, apparently advocated 'a tax on bachelors: a bounty on families, and a baby-show in every parish', quoted in G. Drysdale, *Population Fallacies: a defence of the Malthusian or True Theory of Society*, second edition, London, 1867, p. 18.

an absolute necessity act unnaturally; and the only choice left us is to take the course from which the smallest amount of physical and moral evil will result. It is not with nature that preventive intercourse is to be compared, but with the other necessary checks to population, sexual abstinence, prostitution, and poverty. We have to choose *between* these checks, not independent of them.[33]

Mrs. Besant's defence of the Knowlton pamphlet at the trial of 1877 made the same point.

I must put it to you that men and women, but more especially men, will not lead a celibate life, whether they are married or un-married, and that what you have got to deal with is, that which we advocate—early marriage with restraint upon the numbers of the family—or else a simple mass of unlicensed prostitution, which is the ruin both of men and women when once they fall into it.[34]

It was no part of Knowlton's object

either to destroy marriage, or to favour profligacy, or to promote promiscuous intercourse; but on the contrary, to enable people to marry early, and, at the same time, to avoid those evils which come by over-population.[35]

Indeed, the neo-Malthusians went so far as to argue not only that young men would not, but that they should not abstain for long periods from sexual intercourse. George Drysdale wrote:

The ignorance of the necessity of sexual intercourse to the health and virtue of both man and woman, is the most fundamental error in medical and moral philosophy. A society in which all men and women should restrain their sexual desires till the age of thirty or upwards, would be a scene of such horrible restraint, such absence of manliness and nature, such widespread genital disease, spermatorrhoea, chlorosis, hysteria, and all the allied signs of enfeeblement and morbidity, that it would be next to impossible to find a single healthy or natural individual. If we are to dream of Utopias they should at least be of a somewhat more desirable character.[36]

33. G. Drysdale, *The Elements of Social Science: or Physical, Sexual and Natural Religion,* by a Graduate of Medicine, third edition, enlarged, London, 1860, p. 351. Italics in the original.
34. *The Queen v. C. Bradlaugh and A. Besant,* pp. 64–5.
35. *Ibid.,* p. 110.
36. *Elements of Social Science, op. cit.,* p. 345. Italics in the original. See Robert Dale Owen's earlier assertion, 'Monkish chastity and brutal licence are, equally, the causes of misery and disease', in his *Situations: Lawyers—Clergy—Physicians—Men and Women,* London, 1839, p. 9. Both Annie Besant and Charles Bradlaugh made the same point in their defence, see *Queen v. Bradlaugh and Besant,* pp. 108 and 170–1; and the *Malthusian Handbook,* in 1893, referred to the 'morbid and gloomy celibate', *op. cit.,* p. 12.

The arguments of the neo-Malthusians were received, initially at least, with widespread hostility. There were, indeed, some amongst their critics who rejected the very assumption of over-population, and contended that large families were a blessing rather than a misfortune, holding to the Biblical injunction 'be fruitful and multiply'.[37]

Will they dare to affirm—will they essay to prove—that an increase of population, or an abundance of God's gift in children really means and is attended by a diminution in the supplies and means of support for those children?[38]

In general, however, the majority of those who were concerned with these problems were convinced that large families were no longer desirable either for the nation as a whole, or for individual members of the middle classes, while being equally convinced that 'preventive intercourse' was too dangerous a solution. It was widely believed, as the charge against the Knowlton pamphlet clearly indicates, that the propagation of neo-Malthusian views was 'calculated to deprave public morals'. The precise manner in which this was to be brought about is not always clear from the writings of the critics but there was sufficient plain speaking to bring out certain of the issues on which anxiety was focused. In the first place there was the fear that the spread of contraceptive knowledge would 'tear down one of the greatest protections public morality has'[39] the fear of conception outside marriage. The case for the pro-secution of Bradlaugh and Besant for the publication of the Knowlton pamphlet also rested essentially on these grounds. The Solicitor General told the Jury:

The question for you is, whether a book of this sort, published to everybody, would not suggest to the unmarried as well as to the married, and any persons into whose hands this book might get—the boy of seventeen and the girl of the same age—that they might gratify their passions without the mischief and the inconvenience and the destruction of character which would be involved if they gratified them and conception followed.[40]

37. J. Barker, *A Secret Book for Men*, 1888, p. 45.
38. Blake, *op. cit.* Preface.
39. The *Liverpool Mail*, 23 June, 1877.
40. *The Queen* v. *Bradlaugh and Besant*, pp. 20–21.

Indeed 'the only check against immorality in this country', asserted the counsel for the prosecution in another Neo-Malthusian case fourteen years later, 'is the fear of pregnancy'.[41]

Undoubtedly many were bitterly opposed to the indiscriminate sale of such books at a cheap rate to the general public, while at the same time they condoned if not approved the discreet spread of contraceptive techniques amongst the respectably married. But on the other hand there were many others who genuinely believed that the practice was immoral for married and unmarried alike. With the exception of George Drysdale, the neo-Malthusians were careful to argue that their message was intended for married people, but even if their propaganda could have been restricted in this way there were plenty to declare that 'the essential objection to their doctrines would remain as strong as ever'.[42]

A glance at some of these objections suggests that they were founded on the belief that the practice of birth-control was in fact to yield to man's baser or animal instincts and to surrender the high ideal of purity for the sake of sexual pleasure. Sexual intercourse, according to this view, had as its primary object the propagation of children and pleasure was only 'a secondary consideration'.[43] Yet the principal aim of birth-control techniques was, in contradistinction to moral restraint, to make possible the enjoyment of sexual pleasure while preventing procreation. It is not surprising, therefore, that it should have been opposed by those who emphasized the moral value of self restraint. As they saw it, sexual abstinence was the answer to the problem of over-population and to the whole area of sexual irregularity.

For the evils which arise from over-population and the growth of great cities there is no remedy which the Church can recognize except, on the one hand, in the steady, thoughtful, systematic improvement of the entire social environment of the poor, and on the

---

41. *The Malthusian Handbook: designed to induce married people to limit their families within their means*, 1893, p. 32. The prosecution on this occasion was for the distribution of a leaflet, *Some Reasons for Advocating the Prudential Limitation of Families*.

42. 'John Stuart Mill', *Fraser's Magazine*, November, 1873.

43. T. L. Nichols, *Human Physiology the Basis of Sanitary and Social Science*, London, 1872, p. 298. This book appears to have been written as a reply to Drysdale's *Elements of Social Science*.

other, in the patient inculcation of the laws of prudence and self-restraint.[44]

No choice was open to those who held this view, save between 'young marriages with subsequent abstinence or late marriages with early abstinence.'[45]

Moreover, the opposition to contraception on these grounds continued long after its practice had become a reality. In 1901, it was argued that:

married persons should pray for grace and guidance to exercise that rational self-restraint by which alone—in distinction from the morally shameful and physically harmful practices which have marked effete heathen civilizations and have been re-introduced in our own time and country—either Christian faith or human refinement can aim at prudence in the number of children born.[46]

The neo-Malthusian classification of abstinence as an evil along with profligacy and over-indulgence and hence the argument that recourse to contraception was both medically and morally desirable was met by their opponents with flat rebuttal and with counter-attack. On the one hand they rigorously denied that a young man could not 'lead a chaste life to the age of 25 without injury to his health',[47] and on the other they asserted that practical checks to procreation were both morally and physically dangerous especially to the woman.

Her internal structure fights against the success of unnatural acts; her tissues imbibe any poisonous drug, and resent the absence of what is natural.[48]

At the same time the use of contraception must

44. F. W. Farrar, 'Social Problems and Remedies', the *Fortnightly Review*, March, 1888.

45. 'Population', the *North British Review*, Vol. 8, New Series, December, 1867, No. 94, article 6, p. 456. This article was largely a review of J. M. Duncan's *Fecundity, Fertility, Sterility and Allied Topics*, Edinburgh, 1866, and was reproduced as Part IV, Ch. 4 of the second edition of that work in 1871. The quotation is to be found on p. 267 of that edition.

46. W. J. K. Little, *Holy Matrimony*, London, 1901, p. 222.

47. E. Blackwell, *Counsel to Parents on the Moral Education of their Children, in relation to sex*, second edition revised, London, 1879, p. 63. See also T. L. Nichols, *Human Physiology, op. cit.*, pp. 272–3.

48. F. W. Newman, *The Corruption now called Neo-Malthusianism, op. cit.* See also C. H. F. Routh, *The Moral and Physical Evils likely to Follow if Practices intended to act as Checks to Population be not strongly discouraged and Condemned*, London, 1879.

degrade the finest moral instincts of both men and women, especially
of course, the latter: in them it cannot have any other effect than to
bring about a bestial sensuality and indifference to all morality.[49]

They thus implied that licence, whether indulged in within
marriage or outside it, led inevitably to physical as well as to
moral degradation, and that abstinence was the only solution
to the problems of poverty and prostitution.

This recoil from the dangers of licence and the compensatory
insistence on the virtues of chastity and self-restraint is, perhaps,
one of the most important features of the anti-Malthusian point
of view at this time. And it is significant not merely because
it throws light on the respectable Victorian attitude to sex,
but because it provides us with the key to the central theme of
this study—the relationship of feminism to family size. When
we consider the views of the neo-Malthusians on sexual issues
we cannot find it surprising that there was no support from all
but a tiny minority of feminists for the methods of family
limitation advocated by Charles Bradlaugh and Annie Besant.
As we have seen, the arguments of the neo-Malthusians supported what to their opponents appeared to be nothing but
licentiousness both within marriage and outside it, and although the feminists seem to have shared in the general
'conspiracy of silence' on the issue, it is not unreasonable to
conclude from their views on the broad relationships between
the sexes, that it was in this light that they saw it too. Far from
believing family limitation by means of contraception to be a
further step towards their emancipation, they appear to have
seen it as yet another instance of their subordination to man's
sexual desires.

49. R. Ussher, *Neo-Malthusianism, op. cit.*, 1897, p. 78. The *British Medical
Journal* also believed that such doctrines were 'contrary to the purity of
thought and manliness of life which are the characteristics of this nation.
Dr. Drysdale's doctrines are wholly discountenanced by the medical profession', *B.M.J.*, 26 January, 1878. The reference here, of course, is to Dr.
Charles Robert Drysdale not his brother, Dr. George Drysdale who does
not seem to have been connected in the public mind with the anonymous
Elements of Social Science. See also A. S. Dyer, *Safeguards against Immorality and
Facts that Men Ought to Know*, London, 1884, p. 3, 'The first safeguard
against impurity is to believe in the possibility of self-restraint'. Dyer was
editor of the *Sentinel*, a monthly journal devoted to the advancement of
public morality and the suppression of vice.

Preoccupation of a wife by expected child-birth or by child-nurturing, interferes vexatiously with the wishes of a sexual husband. The philanthropic or economic plea of our False (Neo-) Malthusian is very convenient to such a man—very dangerous to his wife.[50]

The feminist rejection of neo-Malthusianism should, however, be thought of primarily as hostility to family limitation only when brought about by the use of mechanical means. We have no evidence that they were opposed to those methods, either of complete abstinence or possibly of the use of the safe period, which relied on the exercise of self-control in married life. [51] Nor can it be said that they were necessarily hostile to the demand for relief from excessive child-bearing, particularly for working-class women. But, on the other hand, it never formed part of their propaganda; and it may well have been that they feared to be associated in the minds of the public with the 'unsavoury' doctrines of people like Bradlaugh and Besant and George Drysdale, as well as the extreme left wing of the American emancipation movement some of whose members were calling for 'free love'. It also seems possible that to some feminists at least, the desire for smaller families itself was suspect as an aim for the movement, since it came, often enough, from the pleasure-loving woman who had no interest in woman's rights and who was regarded by them as a danger to their own position, because she was so often referred to as the logical outcome of feminist doctrines. In these circumstances we can understand why the cause of family limitation was so pointedly ignored by the great majority of those who were working for the equality of the sexes in the nineteenth century.

50. Newman, op. cit. The periods when 'a woman is physically unable to indulge in love' had long been recognized as one of the 'defects of monogamy' and a cause of prostitution, Walker, op. cit., p. 325.

51. F. Blackwell, Counsel to Parents, op. cit., p. 112. See also the 'advanced' woman writer in the Humanitarian, February, 1894, quoted in R. Ussher, Neo-Malthusianism, op. cit., pp. 97–8.

CHAPTER 9

Emancipation and Family Size

THE establishment of a precise cause and effect sequence is never easy, especially when that sequence is an historical one. In addition to the philosophical difficulties involved in the concept of causation, and the methodological complexities of the analysis of social fact, which the historical sociologist shares with his sociological colleagues, there is the extra burden, shared with the historian proper, of finding in the available sources sufficient material to provide the evidence needed for his purpose. Such a task becomes all the more complicated when the subject matter relates to topics which, because they were considered indecent or immoral, were rarely discussed in public and in consequence have not left vestigial remains in the form of reported conversations, lectures, articles, pamphlets, or books. The approach perforce must be oblique and some attempt must be made to infer the state of contemporary opinion from what was said about allied topics.

In the present instance, for example, census data carefully sifted by demographers has established beyond all reasonable doubt that the English middle-class professional and business men from the 1870's onwards had consistently smaller families than those of a previous generation. We also have strong reasons for believing that this was the consequence of a deliberate choice on their part, the result of a conscious decision to have less children than they might, and not the effect of some decline in their reproductive power or change in their physical environment. We also know that the middle classes themselves long before 1870 expressed the desire to preserve a high standard of living after marriage as their reason for postponing it. What is far more difficult to ascertain is whether there were other motives, more powerful than the economic, which were working to lead them consciously, or unconsciously, to prefer family planning within marriage to the previous alternative of protracted courtships. In particular we are faced—in a situation of scarcity of evidence—with the problem of whether the change occurred because of a new outlook on the part of the wife to assert her independence in matters involving child-birth, or because of an equally new concern on the part of the husband for his wife's well-being in this respect.

What we must assume in all this, of course, is that public statements are an important source of information about private opinion. Although the possibility of hypocrisy always exists in any given instance, it does not make sense to charge a whole generation or a whole class of people with double-dealing. We must accept that most of those whose writings have come down to us believed what they said as they said it, and that they would not readily have committed themselves in print unless they were willing to have their names associated with the views expressed. Nor is it likely that those who were recognized as workers in a movement would have been allowed to commit the movement to views which the majority deplored, without there being some sign of the feeling that they had transgressed. In this sense it is possible to argue from silence; and to make a rough estimate of the strength of an opinion from the extent to which it is repeated in the literature by all kinds of people in all sorts of situations.

Hence, when we argue, in Chapter 2, that the rights of women discussion never achieved the level of a true debate about family limitation, we are comparing the regular flow of books, pamphlets and articles linking the standard of living with family size, and the spasmodic appearance every twenty years or so of a work advocating family limitation as a means to the emancipation of women. Considerations of cost and prudence in contracting marriage were linked in the public mind with the case for and against smaller families. The emancipation of women was not; at least, not until after family limitation was already under way.

We have indeed to beware of a tautology here. Because the twentieth century has seen that, as a matter of fact, smaller families make it possible for women to be emancipated from many of the burdens of child-bearing as well as child-rearing, it is easy to fall into the habit of thinking of the phenomenon itself as a cause. But the argument must mean more than this. It implies that other aspects of emancipation preceded the fall in the birth-rate and were, at least in part, responsible for it, and it is the evidence for precisely these other aspects which is lacking in the period before 1870.

If we consider the feminist movement itself, we find that most of its achievements date from after the 1870's. The vote was still many years away; legislation improving the position of the married woman was confined to the wife living apart from her husband; the professions were still the prerogative of men. Even the extension of higher education, one of the most notable successes of the early feminists, dates mainly from the 1870's and after, when the universities began to open their doors to women and the expansion of girls' secondary education took place. The only exception is the success of the movement for widening the opportunities of employment for those middle-class girls who were forced to earn their own living. These new opportunities were, however, confined to the spinsters and widows. The married woman with a career, at least as far as the middle class are concerned, is largely a twentieth-century innovation other than in certain vocations such as the stage and literature, with which the feminists were not concerned.

Nor can it be said that the feminists were indirectly responsible for the emancipation of the married woman. It might be argued that the possession of economic independence gave the possibility of a choice between marriage and a career, so that some middle-class girls refused to marry except on their own terms. Certainly by the end of the century we can meet examples of the spinster who was unmarried from choice rather than necessity. But this is no evidence for a growing independence within marriage, particularly up to and including the 1870's, when the movement for higher education was in its infancy. Neither does it seem to be associated with the later age of marriage. Rather was it the young man of the middle classes who postponed his proposal of marriage or endured a lengthy courtship while he established himself in his career.

It is moreover, not even plausible to argue that the efforts of the feminists resulted in family planning in the next generation. The suggestion, for example, that those girls who benefited from opportunities for education denied to their mothers restricted their families as a direct consequence of that education, is not supported by the evidence. The number of children born to girls educated at the women's colleges at Oxford and Cambridge did not differ appreciably from the number born to girls of the same class without a college education. Girls who had received some form of higher education were not, it is true, so likely to marry either because the typical middle-class man reacted against the idea of a 'blue stocking' as a wife, or because the college girl preferred to retain her independence; but, once married, she was no more likely than other girls of her class to resort to birth-control.

There is no evidence, therefore, for the argument that the emancipation of women was a causal factor in the fall in fertility so long as we equate the emancipation of women with feminism. It may be, however, that we are wrong to concentrate so exclusively on the concept of revolt. Feminism indeed, whether we conceive it as the struggle for the vote, for education or for a career, was conceived directly as a struggle of the underprivileged female against the dominant, privileged male. Emancipation, if used in this sense, entails a campaign waged in the face of opposition, whether from men or women, for a change in the traditional relationship between the sexes. As applied to family limitation it suggests that women independently, or even against the wishes of their husbands, made the decision to practise birth-control, and where *coitus interruptus* or the condom was the method used, somehow induced their husbands to acquiesce in the idea. Essentially, it implies that women were revolting against an exclusively passive role so far as decisions involving sex and reproduction were concerned. The feminists themselves did not publicly advocate such a campaign, although individual feminists might privately have fought such a battle;[1] and it is most unlikely that the development of family planning could have been the product of a widespread 'revolt' and not left evidence of conflict and protest in the literature.

Middle-class husbands in the 1860's and 1870's, it must be assumed, were willing partners in the new attitude to family size. If emancipation was involved; it was emancipation by

1. Mrs. Besant, for example, testified in her divorce suit 'that her efforts to impress upon her husband their duty to limit their family within their means had been a source of friction between them', G. M. Williams, *The Passionate Pilgrim: a Life of Annie Besant*, 1931, p. 80.

consent—in marked contrast to the goals of the feminists which were fought for every step of the way. Moreover, whatever their motives may have been, there is little evidence that men were willing to practise birth-control or to condone it for the sake of their wives. Doctors on both sides of the neo-Malthusian debate often argued that men should be concerned about the effect of too-frequent child-bearing on the health of the mother, but they implied, and usually asserted, that such a concern was rare. Husbands were self-indulgent sexually and their wives submitted dutifully.[2]

Nor does it seem likely that men were more prepared to limit their families because of the strain of child-rearing on their wives. At this time, domestic servants were plentiful and relatively inexpensive. The middle-class woman had long been emancipated from routine drudgery in the home and employed nursemaids or governesses to look after the children. Only in the sense that the 1870's might be said to have faced the middle classes with problems of *cost* can it be argued that emancipation was involved. In cutting down expenses the middle-class husband preferred to restrict the size of his family rather than force his wife back into the nursery or the kitchen.

It would, however, seem to be more plausible to interpret this preference in terms of the middle-class husband's desire to maintain his standard of living rather than in terms of a concern for his wife's comfort. Long before the 1870's the concept of the perfect wife for the middle classes had entailed the notion of a 'civilized' existence in which the leisured lady was, in Veblen's term, the hall-mark of conspicuous consumption. Just as the keeping of a carriage and the employment of domestic servants, and, later, the education of his sons at Public Schools were the measure of a man's economic progress, so the possession of a leisured, elegant and expensively dressed wife marked him off as more successful than his fellows. To admit defeat to the extent of reducing her to the status of head nurse or head housemaid would appear to have been seen as too drastic a step to take, especially when other means of retrench-

2. See, for example, *The Duties of Parents: Reproductive and Educational*, London, 1872, pp. 30–2. T. L. Nichols, *Esoteric Anthropology (The Mysteries of Man)*, London, 1873, p. 149, and the *North British Review*, December, 1867, pp. 458–9, in a review of J. M. Duncan's *Fecundity, Sterility and Allied Topics*, and quoted in the second edition of that work, Edinburgh, 1871, p. 271.

ment lay to hand. Undoubtedly the wife, accustomed to her genteel role, would have protested too, but the lack of evidence on the issue leads straight to the conclusion that a protest was not called for because the step was never contemplated.

At the same time, we should not ignore the possible significance for the relationship between the married couple of the development of the concept of the perfect lady. In one sense, of course, it is true to think of this as working against emancipation as the feminists understood it, because it made the wife more financially dependent on her husband. Yet the sheer fact that from 'guiding star' of the home, the woman had become an elegant symbol of its opulence to the world and hence perforce was expected to move more freely outside it, suggests that her personal independence was much more fully recognized than it had been earlier. That this was not the intention goes without saying, since it is most unlikely that middle-class men would spend money on domestic servants merely to show recognition of their wife's independence; but once they had come to employ a number of servants and to look upon their wives as expensive articles of fashion, the freer movement of the leisured lady would seem to have been as inevitable as it was unanticipated.

What we have to ask ourselves, therefore, is the question whether this emancipation from the chores of the domestic routine and the greater freedom to move about outside the home unchaperoned, also represented for the wife the acceptance by her husband of the notion that she might be admitted to a greater share in the making of important family decisions than she had been permitted hitherto. More directly we may ask whether family planning now became possible because men found it easier to talk about such matters with their wives, having already become accustomed to a greater measure of joint discussion on other issues. It cannot be claimed that we can answer such questions with the evidence at our disposal. All we can do is to admit that there is no reason to rule out the possibility that this was indeed a feature of the steady spread of the willingness to consider family planning in the 1870's and after. Certainly, the very use of contraceptive techniques implies some minimum level of discussion about sexual matters. Moreover, if women in the late Victorian period were in fact more ready to discuss these matters, however quietly, with their husbands, it must be admitted that the efforts of the feminists may have played a part in this change, albeit in a most unexpected fashion. In their propaganda for the repeal of the Contagious Diseases Acts they familiarized women as well as men with the importance of public debate on sexual questions and so may have prepared the way for a more open discussion in middle-class homes of the issues raised a few years later during the Bradlaugh-Besant trials.

Yet, even were this true, it would not seriously affect the tenor of the argument that a growing participation of the middle-class wife in decisions of this kind, could only have come about in consequence of a change in attitude on the part of her husband, not only to her rights in such matters but also towards family planning generally, and this could have been produced by events far removed from the activities of the feminists. At the same time, in so far as the movement towards the smaller family was linked with a tendency towards earlier marriages, it is possible that it was indirectly influenced by the attitude taken by the feminists towards prostitution. Their share in the attack on the widespread acquiescence in a double standard of sexual morality, and, in particular, the part they played in the campaign for the repeal of the Contagious Diseases Acts may well have made the middle-class bachelor less complacent about his recourse to the prostitute. Indeed, apart altogether from considerations of sexual morality, the campaign must have served to re-emphasize the dangers of venereal disease. It would not be surprising if, in those circumstances, the young middle-class man were to be impressed by the neo-Malthusian literature which constantly reiterated the argument that he could afford an earlier marriage if he would only combine it with family limitation. In the absence of evidence all this must be conjectural, but even supposing it to be correct, it should be emphasized that this result was not at all in line with the intentions of the feminists who hoped by their efforts to promote sexual abstinence both outside and within marriage.

The general impression, therefore, which results from considering those possible influences of feminism for which there is no direct evidence merely confirms the major conclusions of this study. The feminist movement as such was not a causal factor in the advent of family planning, and any of its activities which may validly be linked with this development are to be seen as consequences not only unanticipated, but, if they had been anticipated, almost certainly unapproved.

Conclusion

IT remains to consider whether it is possible to generalize from the particular conclusions of this study in order to establish possible relationships between feminism and family size in conditions other than those of nineteenth-century England. In particular, concern for the future numbers of mankind and for the possibility that we shall soon be faced with starving generations in overcrowded lands has, since World War II, led to active government propaganda and positive measures of assistance to induce people to undertake family planning in several parts of the world. Such programmes have been only partially successful, and we have now to consider whether it is possible to throw some light on their failure from what we have learned about the conditions necessary for a fall in family size from our studies of nineteenth-century English middle-class experiences.

The first point to notice is that it is not at all necessary to have achieved equality between men and women for the acceptance of family planning. So far as we can tell from the literature at our disposal there is no evidence that 'emancipated' women in the feminist sense of the term, once married, had fewer children than those in the same social class who were 'unemancipated' although they were, in the early years of feminism, more likely to stay unmarried. In any case, family planning became established amongst English middle-class families while feminism as an organized movement was in its infancy and while all the evidence points to the initiative in the matter being taken by the man in a society largely dominated by masculine values. In this connection it is interesting to note that a fairly recent study of family planning in Puerto Rico supports the inference that in a male-dominated society it is the men who must be convinced of the necessity of desirability of family planning.

Female modesty inculcated early in childhood makes many women reluctant to bring up such matters; and leads males to conclude that such matters are not for discussion with their wives. Male dominance leads some husbands to believe that the sphere of family planning is their prerogative alone, and makes wives reluctant to initiate conversation or action. Moreover, there is some evidence suggesting that when conversation does occur it tends to be one-sided, i.e. the male talking, the female listening.[1]

A programme of family planning directed to women would, accordingly, not be likely to prove successful. In male-dominated societies women take their cues in such matters from the men.[2]

This may perhaps explain why the government efforts in India have so far been largely unsuccessful. In 1951 the Government of India Planning Commission advocated family planning on two counts.

While Family Planning is intended to bring down over a period of time the rate of population growth, immediately it is a step in the direction of improvement in health, especially of mothers and children.[3]

At this time Professor Chandrasekhar believed that it would not be a difficult task to

enlighten the public mind in India as to the benefits of birth-control. Once the public health officials begin hammering in its importance, it will spread even to the traditionally forgotten villages. Once Indian mothers are educated in the right belief that there is a scientific device to meet their desperate, albeit latent demands, birth-control can easily make headway.[4]

Yet, eight years later we are told that contraception is making very slow progress in India, as it is in Japan.[5] It is, of course, not at all unlikely that the sheer physical difficulties mentioned by India's population experts, such as the poor housing con-

1. J. M. Stycos, K. Back and R. Hill, 'Problems of Communication between Husband and Wife on Matters Relating to Family Limitation', *Human Relations*, Vol. 9, No. 2, May 1956, p. 214.
2. J. Blake, 'Family Instability and Reproductive Behaviour in Jamaica', in *Current Research in Human Fertility, Papers Presented at the 1954 Annual Conference of the Milbank Memorial Fund*, New York, 1955.
3. Government of India Planning Commission, *The First Five-Year Plan—a Draft Outline*, New Delhi, 1951, p. 206.
4. S. Chandrasekhar, *Hungry People and Empty Lands*, Allen and Unwin, London, 1954, p. 191. The preface is dated June, 1952.
5. R. A. Gopalaswami, 'How Japan Halved her Birth-Rate in Ten Years and the Lessons for India', *Population Review: A Journal of Asian Demography*, Vol. 3, No. 2, July, 1959. The Japanese 'solution' was largely achieved through a tremendous increase in the incidence of abortion.

ditions of most Indian families, have their part to play in in-
hibiting the use of contraceptives, but, nevertheless, what is
usually referred to by them as the traditionalist attitude towards family planning would seem to be crucial.

It is here that we should emphasize the middle-class nature
of our study of feminism and family planning. In the British
context working-class family planning was of a later date and is
usually regarded as an example of 'cultural diffusion', working-
class families taking the lead from those slightly above them in
social status. Recent neo-Malthusian propaganda in so-called
under-developed areas, on the other hand, is addressed to whole
populations, and the standards people are expected to adopt
are not so much those of their own middle classes, but those of
the Western industrial communities. The kind of cultural
diffusion called for is much more radical, and we should hesitate to generalize simply from nineteenth-century experience.
Nevertheless, it is of some interest to learn that in an Indian
village which was studied for the light it might throw on factors
relating to traditionalistic attitudes towards family planning,
willingness to make use of contraceptives on the part of the
men was directly related to the amount of education they had
received, as measured by the number of years of schooling.[6]
In so far as exposure to the conditioning process of education may
be taken as in some ways the characteristic feature of differences
between middle-class and working-class men in nineteenth-
century England, and in some respect, responsible for differences between them in terms of their appreciation of the level
of living necessary for a 'reasonably civilized' existence, the
study suggests that family planners in over-populated areas
might concentrate their attentions on raising the standards to
be expected from life on the part of men in such societies.
We might, that is to say, draw the general conclusion from
Feminism and Family Planning, as from *Prosperity and Parenthood*,
that the important issue is the man's attitude towards his family
as part of what he should struggle to achieve in material term.

At the same time, we should not ignore the possible significance of the emancipation of women from their purely domestic

6. W. A. Morrison, 'Attitude of Males Toward Family Planning in A
Western Indian Village', *Milbank Memorial Fund Quarterly*, Vol. 34, No. 3,
July, 1956.

role. In the Victorian middle-class context this meant, as we have seen, that the housewife became a lady of leisure. Clearly, this does not apply to the working-classes for whom there was no question of the employment of domestic servants to make it possible. Nevertheless, there is something to be said for the view that women, whatever their social class or cultural background, are more likely themselves to accept the idea of family limitation when they are no longer valued only as mothers, and when they can derive satisfaction, and status, from other activities, whatever these may be. While the available evidence suggests that this is not one of the main factors in the fall in family size, it may be inevitably linked with others that are, and hence appear as a contributory factor.

Finally, we may consider whether it is possible to generalize from our findings with respect to the nature of nineteenth-century feminism. Family planning, we argue, may and does occur in the absence of feminist support, but it does not follow that this support must always be withheld. In terms of the material presented in this study, Victorian middle-class feminists had their own special approach to the whole issue of sexual relationships which, it may be assumed, arose primarily from roots in Christian puritanism. Feminists in other parts of the world, seeking to equalize the status of men and women, especially if their traditional background derives from a very different set of religious beliefs, might regard neo-Malthusian practices as furthering, rather than undermining, the 'true' interests of women. As against this we have to consider whether feminists everywhere have been obliged to combat a double standard of sexual morality and to ask whether in such circumstances they might always be inclined to see family limitation, for which the initiative is taken by men, as but another example of the insidiousness of that standard.

It is evident that we cannot do more here than mention possible generalizations which occur from this study, together with any practical implications to be drawn from them. What is required now is further research into the nature of the actual movement towards the smaller family in different parts of the world, and further research into twentieth-century feminist movements, where these are not merely repeating the shibboleths of the past but have developed new ideas to meet the problems of a new generation. It can only be through the cumulative effort of researches of this kind that we shall come closer to understanding the factors which have led to family limitation in the Western world and the problems which confront those who seek to control population increases in Africa and the East.

APPENDIX

List of Relevant Books and Pamphlets on the Woman Question, published in Britain in the Period, 1792 to 1880

The following list is intended to cover the period of the genesis and development of the Malthusian controversy in Britain (see the introduction to the List of Books, Pamphlets, and Articles on the Population Question, published in Britain in the Period 1793 to 1880, compiled by J. A. Banks and D. V. Glass, and published in D. V. Glass, ed. *Introduction to Malthus*, Watts, London, 1953, pp. 81–83). Hence it contains only those writings on the status of women which are relevant to that controversy. Books and pamphlets on other aspects of feminism, such as those on the legal position of women, the education of girls, or the extension of the franchise, where they have contained no references to the family or to population questions, have not been included. Articles in magazines and newspapers have also been ignored, except where they were republished in book or pamphlet form. It is not pretended that this list is complete, although every attempt was made initially to identify all sources which seemed likely to be useful. Its main purpose is to provide a larger coverage of the data used to obtain the general impression of the relationship between feminism and family planning described in the earlier chapters of this book, than it is possible to provide there without overburdening the text; but at the same time it is hoped that it will be useful to students of population who wish to extend the 1953 list on the Malthusian controversy, and to students of feminism who are anxious to set that topic in the general context of the opinion of the day. It may also be read in terms of the general methodological conviction that the only way the historical sociologist can satisfactorily comply with the requirements of systematic enquiry in the field of opinion studies, is to provide a complete list of the contemporary sources which have been used so that other students in the field may test for themselves how far the conclusions reached are validly based. For convenience the list is arranged in chronological order by the first edition of the cited work where the date of this is known.

Apart from the earlier list on the population question and from the other publications listed in the introduction to it, the only bibliographical aid which has been of use in preparing this Appendix is the 'British Bibliography on Women's Questions' published seriatim through several issues in the *Englishwoman's Review* in 1899. Since this is not generally available, the full details may be of value.

16th January, 1899	I History and Essays on General Aspects, 1545–1893.
	II Law, 1632–1893.
	III Parliamentary Enfranchisement, 1825–72.
15th April, 1899	III Parliamentary Enfranchisement, 1872–99.
15th July, 1899	IV Poor Law and Local Government Work, 1859–79.
16th October, 1899	IV Poor Law and Local Government Work, 1880–94.
	V Employment, 1843–99.
	VI Medicine, 1876–95.
	VII Education, 1787–1898.
	VIII Biographical and Miscellaneous, 1803–98.

The *Englishwoman's Review* also published a list on the suffrage movement up to and including the 1870's, in the issue of 14th December, 1889, and a list of journals on women's questions in the issue of 16th July, 1900.

Wollstonecraft, Mary: *A Vindication of the Rights of Women, with Strictures on Political and Moral Subjects*, London, 1792, 2nd ed. Boston, 1792, 3rd ed. (Preface, W. Strange) London, 1844.

Gregory, John: *A Father's Legacy to his Daughters*, London, 1774, editions 1775, 1778, New ed. 1784, 1788, 1789, 1790, 1793 (?), Paris, 1800, 1801, 1808, 1809, 1810, 1812, 1816, 1822, 1828, 1868, 1877.

Gisbourne, Thomas: *An Inquiry into the Duties of the Female Sex*, London, 1797, 2nd ed., corrected, London, 1797, 3rd ed., corrected, London, 1798, 5th ed., London, 1801, 7th ed., corrected, London, 1806, 8th ed., corrected, London, 1810.

Anon: *An Appeal to the Men of Great Britain, in Behalf of Women*, London, 1798, (reviewed in the *Gentleman's Magazine*, April, 1799, Vol. 69, Pt. I), (Authoress prob. Mary Hays, see Thompson's *Appeal* (p. vii) or Mrs. Mary Hay, see D. M. Stenton, *The English Woman in History*, 1957, p. 319, p. 6.)

Wakefield, Priscilla: *Reflections on the Present Conditions of the Female Sex, with Suggestions for its Improvement*, London, 1798, 2nd ed. London, 1817.

More, Hannah: *Strictures on the Modern System of Female Education, with a view of the Principles and Conduct Prevalent among Women of Rank and Fortune*, 3rd ed., London, 1799, 5th ed., London, 1799, 8th ed., London, 1800, 10th ed., London, 1806, 11th ed., London, 1811.

Radcliffe, Mary Ann: *The Female Advocate or an Attempt to recover the Rights of Women from Usurpation*, London, 1799, Edinburgh, 1810.

Randall, Anne-Frances: *A letter to the Women of England, on the Injustice of Mental Subordination; with anecdotes*, London, 1799, (reviewed in the *Gentleman's Magazine*, April, 1799, Vol. 69, Pt. I).

Hamilton, Elizabeth: *Letters addressed to the Daughters of a Nobleman, or the Formation of Religious and Moral Principle*, 2 vols., 2nd ed., London, 1806, 2 vols., 3rd ed., London, 1814.

Moore, Theophilus: *Marriage Customs and Modes of Courtship of the Various Nations of the Universe, with remarks on the Condition of Women, Penn's maxims, and Counsel to the Single and Married, etc., etc.*, London, 1814, 2nd ed., London, 1820.

Taylor, Ann: *Maternal Solicitude for a Daughter's best interests*, 3rd ed., London, 1814, 5th ed., London, 1816, 10th ed., London, 1822, 11th ed., London, 1824, 12th ed., London, 1825, New ed., enlarged, London, 1855.

Taylor, Ann: *Practical Hints to Young Females, on the Duties of a Wife, a Mother, and a Mistress of a Family*, London, 1815, 6th ed., London, 1816, 11th ed., London, 1822.

Hamilton, Augusta: *Marriage Rites, Customs and Ceremonies of the Nations of the Universe*, London, 1822.

Thompson, William: *Appeal of one half of the human race, women, against the pretensions of the other half, men, to retain them in political, and thence in civil and domestic, slavery; in reply to a paragraph of Mr. Mill's celebrated 'Article on Government'*, London, 1825.

Sandford, Mrs. John: *Women in her Social and Domestic Character*, London, 1831, 2nd ed., London, 1833, 6th ed., London, 1839, (reviewed in the *Edinburgh Review*, Vol. 73, No. 147, April, 1841).

Anon: *Woman as she is, and as she should be*, London, 1835.

Sandford, Mrs. John (Elizabeth): *Female Improvement*, London, 1836, 2nd ed., London, 1839, 3rd ed., London, 1848 (reviewed in the *Edinburgh Review*, Vol. 73, No. 147, April, 1841).

Ellis, Mrs. Sarah (née Stickney): *The Women of England: their Social Duties and Domestic Habits*, London, 1838, 13th ed., London, 1839,

1843, 1844, 1846, (reviewed in the *Edinburgh Review*, Vol. 73, No. 147, April, 1841).

Anon: *Woman as Virgin, Wife, and Mother*, London, 1838.

Walker, Alexander: *Women physiologically examined as to mind, morals, matrimonial slavery, infidelity and divorce*, London, 1839, 2nd ed., London, 1840.

Anon: *Woman's Mission*, 2nd ed., London, 1839, 8th ed., London, 1840, 14th ed., London, 1861, (reviewed in the *Edinburgh Review*, Vol. 73, No. 147, April, 1841).

Morgan, Lady Sydney (née Owenson): *Woman and her Master*, 2 vols., London, 1840, (1st volume only reviewed in the *Edinburgh Review*, Vol. 73, No. 147, April, 1841).

Anon: *Woman's Rights and the Wife at Home by A Womanly Woman*, London, 1840.

Anon: *Woman's Rights and Duties considered with relation to their influence on Society and on her own condition: by a woman*, London, 1840.

Philanthropist: *Domestic Tyranny, or, Women in Chains, with an inquiry as to the best mode of breaking her bonds asunder, and securing her, in lieu thereof, the more effectual links of mutual respect and co-operation*, London, 1841.

Parsons, Benjamin: *The Mental and Moral Dignity of Women*, London, 1842.

Ellis, Mrs. Sarah (née Stickney): *The Mothers of England, their Influence and Responsibility*, London, 1843, new ed., London, 1860.

Ellis, Mrs. Sarah (née Stickney): *The Wives of England, their Relative Duties, Domestic Influence and Social Obligations*, London, 1843, 1846, 1850.

H. G. C. (Muzzey, Artemas Bowers): *The English Maiden: her moral and domestic duties*, London, 1843.

Muzzey, Artemas Bowers: *The Young Maiden*, London, 1843.

Reid, Mrs. Hugo: *A Plea for Women; being a Vindication of the Importance and Extent of her Natural Sphere of Action: with remarks on Recent Works on the Subject*, Edinburgh, 1843, New ed., 1850.

Anon: *Woman an Enigma: or, Life and its Revealings*, London, 1843.

Dryden, Anne Richelieu (née Lamb): *Can Woman Regenerate Society?* London, 1844.

Anon: *Woman's Worth: or Hints to Raise the Female Character*, 2nd ed., London, 1844.

Ellis, Mrs. Sarah (née Stickney): *The Daughters of England, their Position in Society, Character and Responsibilities*, London, 1845, new ed., London, 1846.

Anon: *Woman; her character and vicissitudes*, London, 1845.

Grey, Maria, Georgina, and Shireff, Emily, A. E.: *Thoughts on*

Self-Culture, addressed to Women, London, 1850, 2nd ed., London, 1854.

Milne, John Duguid: *Industrial and Social Position of Women in the Middle and Lower Ranks*, London, 1857, 2nd ed., London, 1870.

Strutt, Elizabeth: *The Feminine Soul, its Nature and Attributes*, London, 1857.

(Craik, Dinah Maria (née Mulock)): *A Woman's Thoughts about Women*, London, 1858.

Landels, William: *Woman's Sphere and Work, considered in the light of scripture*, London, 1859.

Le Plus Bas: *Woman's Rights and Woman's Wrongs, a dying legacy*, London, 1859, 1865.

Cobbe, Frances Power: *Essays on the Pursuits of Woman. Reprinted from Fraser's and MacMillan's Magazines. Also a paper on female education, read before the Social Science Congress*, London, 1863.

Hodgson, William Ballantyre: *The Education of Girls: and the employment of women of the upper classes educationally considered, two lectures*, London, 1866, 2nd ed., London, 1869.

Anon: *The Social and Political Dependence of Women*, London, 1867, 2nd ed., London, 1867.

Anon: *A Woman's View of Woman's Rights*, London, 1867.

Anon: *Female Franchise. Have Women Immortal Souls? The Popular Belief Disputed. By a Clerk in Holy Orders*, London, 1868.

(Taylor, Harriet and Mill, John Stuart): *The Enfranchisement of Women*, London, 1868, (reprinted from the *Westminster and Foreign Quarterly Review*, Vol. 55, July 1851).

Butler, Josephine Elizabeth: ed. *Women's Work and Women's Culture: a Series of Essays*, London, 1869.

Linton, Eliza (née Lynn): *Ourselves: A Series of Essays on Women*, London, 1869, 2nd ed., London, 1870.

Mill, John Stuart: *The Subjection of Women*, London, 1869.

Sewell, Mrs. Sarah Ann: *Woman and the Times we live in*, 2nd ed., Manchester, 1869.

Landels, William: *Woman: her position and power*, London, 1870.

Taylor, Mary: *The First Duty of Woman*, London, 1870.

Janus: *Why Women cannot be Turned into Men*, Edinburgh, 1872.

Stephen, James Fitzjames: *Liberty, Equality, Fraternity*, London, 1873, 2nd ed., London, 1874.

Fawcett, Millicent (née Garrett Anderson): *Mr. Fitzjames Stephen on the Position of Women*, London, 1873, (reprinted from the *Examiner*).

Anon: *Woman: her true place and standing: an address by an American Clergyman*, Edinburgh, 1875.

Anon: *Woman's Work: A Woman's Thoughts on Women's Rights,* London, 1876.

Yonge, Charlotte Mary: *Womankind,* 1876.

Shillito, Joseph: *Womanhood: its duties, temptations and privileges,* London, 1877.

(Ishe): *Woman's True Power and Rightful Work,* London, 1878.

Adams, William Henry Davenport: *Woman's Work and Worth in Childhood, Maidenhood, and Wifehood,* London, 1879.

Index

Abortion, 69, 86–7, 131n
Anti-feminism, 10, 42–57, 95–6, 104, 108–9

Besant, Annie, 88–94, 97, 116, 120, 125n
Birth control:
  acceptance of, 83, 87–8, 91–2, 122, 127
  attitude of the Church to, xi, 98–100, 118–19, 133
  attitude of the feminists to, 24–6, 92–7, 100–3, 120
  attitude of the medical profession to, xi, 98, 119–20
  early advocacy of, 20–1, 25
  propaganda in the 1860's, 25, 85, 88
  (See also Bradlaugh-Besant trial, Neo-Malthusianism)
Blackwell, Elizabeth, 35, 93, 119, 121
Bradlaugh, Charles, 6, 88–94, 120
Bradlaugh-Besant trial, 82, 88–94, 116–17
Butler, Josephine, 94–6, 109–11

Caird, Mona, 41, 100–1
Careers for women (see employment of women, marriage)
Charitable effort, 32, 40, 51
Children, care of, 63–5, 78–9
Cobbe, Frances, 44, 48, 103–4
Contagious Diseases Acts, 94–7, 109–11, 128

Divorce Law reform, 32, 39, 52–3, 107
Domestic servants, 62–9, 72–4, 126
Double standard (see sex morality)
Drysdale, George, 115–16, 118, 120n

Education of girls:
  campaign for, 9, 16, 23, 35–7, 47–8, 66–7
  effect on family size, 105, 124–5
Ellis, Sarah, 23, 25, 58–62, 68

Emancipation of women:
  effect on family size, 11–13, 54, 67–70, 105, 123–5
  relation to feminism, 11, 54–7, 104–5, 124–5
Emigration, 28–9, 31, 33
Employment of women:
  effect on family size, 50–1
  promotion of, 23–4, 30–8, 81–2
Expenditure, conspicuous, 11–12, 67, 75–8, 126–7

Family limitation (see birth control, education of girls, emancipation of women, employment of women, feminism, Neo-Malthusianism, population trends, standard of living)
Feminine character, ideal of, 22–3, 46–8, 59–60, 82, 108–9 (see also motherhood, ideal of, wife, ideal of)
Feminism:
  as a cause of fertility decline, 5–7, 9–14, 53–7, 120–1, 124–5, 130–4
  in the twentieth century, xii, 9, 112–13, 133–4
  nature of, 8–11, 13–14, 40–1, 121, 125
  (see also birth control, education of girls, emancipation of women, employment of women, household duties)

Gentility, 12–13, 71–84, 115, 126–7

Historical sociology, methodology of, 1–14, 122–4, 135
Home, ideal of, 58–9, 65–6, 74, 108–9
Household duties:
  alleged neglect of, 43–6, 56, 66, 68, 105
  attitude of feminists to, 19, 41, 44, 48–50, 66–8
  content of, 62–5